OpenCV Android Programming By Example

Develop vision-aware and intelligent Android applications with the robust OpenCV library

Amgad Muhammad

BIRMINGHAM - MUMBAI

OpenCV Android Programming By Example

First published: December 2015

Production reference: 1071215

Published by Packt Publishing Ltd.
Livery Place
35 Livery Street
Birmingham B3 2PB, UK.

ISBN 978-1-78355-059-3

www.packtpub.com

Credits

Author
Amgad Muhammad

Reviewers
Noritsuna Imamura

André Moreira

Commissioning Editor
Neil Alexander

Acquisition Editor
Meeta Rajani

Content Development Editor
Mayur Pawanikar

Technical Editor
Manthan Raja

Copy Editor
Tasneem Fatehi

Project Coordinator
Nidhi Joshi

Proofreader
Safis Editing

Indexer
Monica Ajmera Mehta

Graphics
Ahmed H. Alley

Kirk D'Penha

Jason Monteiro

Production Coordinator
Arvindkumar Gupta

Cover Work
Arvindkumar Gupta

About the Author

Amgad Muhammad has a master's degree in computer science from the American University in Cairo. He is a data scientist passionate about building and designing machine learning models and engineering features in computer vision research. He started working with computer vision in 2011, and now he is developing state-of-the-art machine learning and computer vision algorithms in the field of biometric extraction and registration, including face and person detection, human tracking, and 2D/3D-based pose estimation.

First, I would like to thank my lovely wife, Noha, and my beautiful kids, Zain, Hla, and Darine, for their continuous care so that I could finish this book. The book is the fruit of my family's support and understanding, in spite of all the time it took me away from them, and all the weekends I spent in front of my computer. It was really a challenging and long journey, having a full-time job and my graduate studies while writing this book, but, as a loving and caring family, we were able to pull through.

I would also like to thank my best friend, Ahmed Hassan Alley, for the beautiful graphics and illustrations. And I would like to thank Mayur Pawanikar, Manthan Raja, and Meeta Rajani for helping me throughout the editing process; they made it really easy.

About the Reviewers

Noritsuna Imamura is a specialist in embedded Linux/Android-based computer vision, and is one of the main members of SIProp.org (`http://www.siprop.org/`). His main works are as follows:

- ITRI Smart Glass, which is similar to Google Glass. He worked on this using Android 4.3 and OpenCV 2.4 in June 2014 (`https://www.itri.org.tw/chi/Content/techTransfer/tech_tran_cont.aspx?&SiteID=1&MmmID=620622510147005345&Keyword=&MSid=4858`).

- Treasure Hunting Robot, a brainwave-controlled robot that he developed in February 2012 (`http://www.siprop.org/en/2.0/index.php?product%2FTreasureHuntingRobot`).

- OpenCV for the Android NDK, which has been included since Android 4.0.1 (`http://tools.oesf.biz/android-4.0.1_r1.0/search?q=SIProp`).

- Auto Chasing Turtle, a human face recognition robot with Kinect, which he developed in February 2011 (`http://www.siprop.org/ja/2.0/index.php?product%2FAutoChasingTurtle`).

- Feel Sketch, an AR authoring tool and AR browser as an Android application, which he developed in December 2009 (`http://code.google.com/p/feelsketch/`).

He can be contacted via e-mail at `noritsuna@siprop.org`.

André Moreira received his master's degree in computer science from Pontifical Catholic University of Rio de Janeiro, Brazil in 2015. Currently he is PhD candidate in the same university.

He graduated with a bachelor's degree in computer science from Universidade Federal do Maranhão (UFMA) in Brazil. During his undergraduate degree, he was a member of Labmint's research team and worked with medical imaging, specifically breast cancer detection and diagnosis using image processing.

Currently, he works as a researcher and system analyst at Instituto Tecgraf, one of the major research and development labs in computer graphics in Brazil. He has been working extensively with PHP, HTML, and CSS since 2007. Nowadays, he develops projects in C++11/C++14, along with SQLite, Qt, Boost, and OpenGL. More information about him can be acquired on his personal website at www.andredsm.com.

www.PacktPub.com

Support files, eBooks, discount offers, and more

For support files and downloads related to your book, please visit www.PacktPub.com.

Did you know that Packt offers eBook versions of every book published, with PDF and ePub files available? You can upgrade to the eBook version at www.PacktPub.com and as a print book customer, you are entitled to a discount on the eBook copy. Get in touch with us at service@packtpub.com for more details.

At www.PacktPub.com, you can also read a collection of free technical articles, sign up for a range of free newsletters and receive exclusive discounts and offers on Packt books and eBooks.

https://www2.packtpub.com/books/subscription/packtlib

Do you need instant solutions to your IT questions? PacktLib is Packt's online digital book library. Here, you can search, access, and read Packt's entire library of books.

Why subscribe?
- Fully searchable across every book published by Packt
- Copy and paste, print, and bookmark content
- On demand and accessible via a web browser

Free access for Packt account holders

If you have an account with Packt at www.PacktPub.com, you can use this to access PacktLib today and view 9 entirely free books. Simply use your login credentials for immediate access.

To my wife, Noha, and my children, Zain, Hla, and Darine

Table of Contents

Preface

Learn how to use OpenCV to develop vision-aware, intelligent Android applications in a step-by-step tutorial and join the interesting and rapidly expanding field of computer vision to enable your Android phone to make sense of the world.

Starting from the basics of computer vision and OpenCV, we'll take you through all the ways to create exciting applications. You will discover that although computer vision is a challenging subject, the ideas and algorithms used are simple and intuitive, and you will appreciate the abstraction layer that OpenCV offers in order to do the heavy lifting for you.

Packed with many examples, the book will help you understand the main data structures used in OpenCV, and how you can use them to gain performance boosts. Next, we will discuss and use several image processing algorithms, such as histogram equalization, filters, and color space conversion. You then will learn about image gradients and how they are used in many shape analysis techniques, such as edge detection, Hough line transform, and Hough circle transform. In addition to using shape analysis to find things in images, you will learn how to describe objects in images in a more robust way using different feature detectors and descriptors. Finally, you will be able to make intelligent decisions using machine learning, specifically, the famous adaptive boosting learning algorithm and cascade classifiers.

What this book covers

Chapter 1, Getting Yourself Ready, explains how to start using OpenCV to develop vision-aware Android applications in a step-by-step fashion.

Chapter 2, App 1 - Building Your Own Darkroom, shows you how images are stored and represented in OpenCV, and how to utilize this representation to implement interesting algorithms that will enhance the way your images look.

Chapter 3, App 2 - Software Scanner, explains how to implement your next application, a software scanner. It allows people to take a photo of, let's say, a receipt, and apply some transformations to make it look as if it was scanned. In this chapter, we will introduce two important topics that will help us to reach our final goal.

The first topic will be about spatial filtering and its definition and applications. The second topic will be about a famous shape analysis technique called the Hough transform. You will learn about the basic idea behind this technique that has made it very popular and widely used, and we will use the OpenCV implementation to start fitting lines and circles to a set of edge pixels.

Chapter 4, App 2 - Applying Perspective Correction, continues to build on the application that we started in Chapter 3. We will use the concepts that you've learned, namely, the edge detection and Hough line transform, to do perspective correction to a quadrilateral object. Applying perspective transformation to an object will change the way that we see it; this idea will come in handy when you take pictures of documents, receipts, and so on, and you want to a have better view of the captured image or a scan-like copy.

Chapter 5, App 3 - Panoramic Viewer, starts working on a new application. The goal of the application is to stitch two images together in order to form a panoramic view, and in this chapter, we will introduce the concept of image features and why they are important, and we will see them in action.

Chapter 6, App 4 – Automatic Selfie, introduces a new application. The goal of the application is to be able to take a selfie without touching your phone's screen. Your application will be able to detect a certain hand gesture that will trigger the process of saving the current camera frame.

What you need for this book

- Tegra Android Development Pack
- An IDE of your choice (Eclipse or Android Studio)
- Android SDK
- Android NDK
- OpenCV4Android SDK

Who this book is for

If you are an Android developer and want to know how to implement vision-aware applications using OpenCV, then this book is definitely for you.

It would be very helpful if you understand the basics of image processing and computer vision, but no prior experience is required.

Conventions

In this book, you will find a number of text styles that distinguish between different kinds of information. Here are some examples of these styles and an explanation of their meaning.

Code words in text, database table names, folder names, filenames, file extensions, pathnames, dummy URLs, user input, and Twitter handles are shown as follows: "To uninstall the previous installation, go to the previous installation directory and run `tadp_uninstall.exe`."

A block of code is set as follows:

```
LOCAL_PATH := $(call my-dir)
include $(CLEAR_VARS)
LOCAL_MODULE    := hello-jni
LOCAL_SRC_FILES := hello-jni.c
```

When we wish to draw your attention to a particular part of a code block, the relevant lines or items are set in bold:

```
Mat rgbImage=new Mat();

Imgproc.cvtColor(originalImage, rgbImage, Imgproc.COLOR_BGR2RGB);
```

New terms and **important words** are shown in bold. Words that you see on the screen, for example, in menus or dialog boxes, appear in the text like this: "You will need to choose the type of the installation. Select a custom installation and click **Next**."

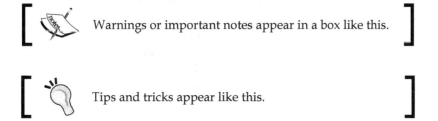

> Warnings or important notes appear in a box like this.

> Tips and tricks appear like this.

Reader feedback

Feedback from our readers is always welcome. Let us know what you think about this book—what you liked or disliked. Reader feedback is important for us as it helps us develop titles that you will really get the most out of.

To send us general feedback, simply e-mail feedback@packtpub.com, and mention the book's title in the subject of your message.

If there is a topic that you have expertise in and you are interested in either writing or contributing to a book, see our author guide at www.packtpub.com/authors.

Customer support

Now that you are the proud owner of a Packt book, we have a number of things to help you to get the most from your purchase.

Downloading the example code

You can download the example code files from your account at http://www.packtpub.com for all the Packt Publishing books you have purchased. If you purchased this book elsewhere, you can visit http://www.packtpub.com/support and register to have the files e-mailed directly to you.

Downloading the color images of this book

We also provide you with a PDF file that has color images of the screenshots/diagrams used in this book. The color images will help you better understand the changes in the output. You can download this file from: https://www.packtpub.com/sites/default/files/downloads/0593OS_ColorImages.pdf.

Errata

Although we have taken every care to ensure the accuracy of our content, mistakes do happen. If you find a mistake in one of our books—maybe a mistake in the text or the code—we would be grateful if you could report this to us. By doing so, you can save other readers from frustration and help us improve subsequent versions of this book. If you find any errata, please report them by visiting http://www.packtpub.com/submit-errata, selecting your book, clicking on the **Errata Submission Form** link, and entering the details of your errata. Once your errata are verified, your submission will be accepted and the errata will be uploaded to our website or added to any list of existing errata under the Errata section of that title.

To view the previously submitted errata, go to `https://www.packtpub.com/books/content/support` and enter the name of the book in the search field. The required information will appear under the **Errata** section.

Piracy

Piracy of copyrighted material on the Internet is an ongoing problem across all media. At Packt, we take the protection of our copyright and licenses very seriously. If you come across any illegal copies of our works in any form on the Internet, please provide us with the location address or website name immediately so that we can pursue a remedy.

Please contact us at `copyright@packtpub.com` with a link to the suspected pirated material.

We appreciate your help in protecting our authors and our ability to bring you valuable content.

Questions

If you have a problem with any aspect of this book, you can contact us at `questions@packtpub.com`, and we will do our best to address the problem.

1
Getting Yourself Ready

In this chapter, I will explain, in a step-by-step fashion, how to start using **OpenCV** to develop vision-aware Android applications.

The **Open Source Computer Vision (OpenCV)** software library has over 2,500 optimized algorithms; the library includes a comprehensive set of both classic and state of the-art computer vision and machine learning algorithms. It has been around for a decade and released under the **Berkeley Software Distribution (BSD)** license, making it easy for users to utilize and modify the code.

OpenCV is downloaded over seven million times and used by well-established companies such as Google, Yahoo, Microsoft, Intel, IBM, Sony, and Honda. Moreover, OpenCV supports several desktop and mobile operating systems including Windows, Linux, Mac OS X, Android, and iOS.

In this book, we will work with OpenCV for Android, which is a part of OpenCV that runs on the Android operating system.

I'll be covering two scenarios for the installation and to get ready; first, if you are starting a clean installation for Android, it is recommended that you start with **Tegra Android Development Pack (TADP)**. The other scenario is a manual setup of every component needed to run Android with OpenCV. You would probably go with this option if you already have a previous installation of the Android development environment. We will cover the following topics:

- Installing Tegra Android Development Pack
- Installing the OpenCV and Android development environment manually
- Understanding how **Native Development Kit (NDK)** works
- Building your first Android project with OpenCV

Installing Tegra Android Development Pack

TADP was released by NVIDIA to make the preparation for the Android development environment a seamless process.

NVIDIA has released TADP version 3.0r4 to support Android SDK (23.0.2), NDK (r10c), and OpenCV for Tegra 2.4.8.2, which is a regular OpenCV4Android SDK extended with Tegra-specific optimizations.

Downloading and installing TADP

To get TADP, visit `https://developer.nvidia.com/tegra-android-development-pack` and follow the steps to become a registered developer; it is a free membership.

Once you have your membership activated, log in and download the version corresponding to your operating system. NVIDIA supports the following operating systems:

- Windows 64-bit
- Mac OS X
- Ubuntu Linux (32/64-bit)

In my case, I have Windows 7 64-bit on my machine, so from now on, all the upcoming steps are tested and working fine on this operating system. However, I don't expect any major changes if you are working with a different operating system.

 For the Ubuntu installation, TADP will need you to have root privileges, so make sure that you do.

Once you finish downloading the TADP installer, launch it and perform the following steps:

1. Follow the onscreen instructions after you read and accept the license agreement.

2. You will need to choose the type of installation. Select a **Custom** installation and click on the **Next** button:

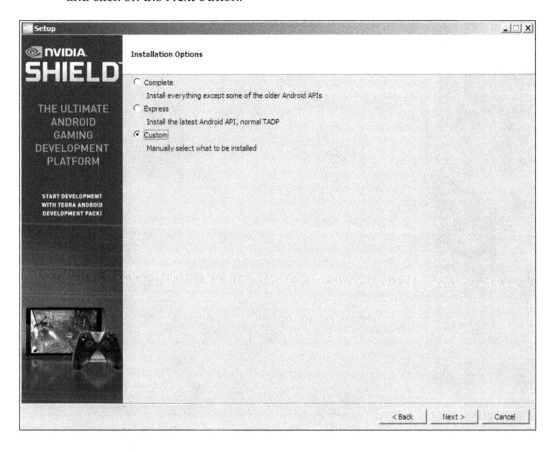

3. Select the components to be installed as depicted and click on the **Next** button:

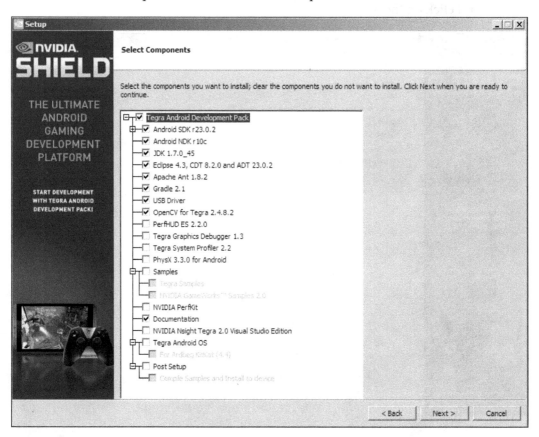

4. You need to name the installation and download the directory.

 Note that if you have a previous installation, you will get a warning message that the previous installation needs to be uninstalled. To uninstall the previous installation, go to the previous installation directory and run `tadp_uninstall.exe`.

Sometimes, the uninstaller doesn't clean everything. In this case, you need to delete the contents of the previous installation directory manually.

5. Now you are ready to install the selected components. Click on the **Next** button.

6. In case you are behind a proxy, you can enter the proxy details; otherwise, click on the **Next** button.

7. The installer will start to download all the selected components; this may take a while depending on your Internet connection.

8. After the download has finished, click **Next** to start installing the selected components.

 Sometimes, the installer window will not respond; this is okay. After a few minutes, the installation will continue in a normal way.

9. Select the post-installation action that you want and click on the **Finish** button.

TADP post-installation configuration

Yes, TADP will download and install everything for you; yet you still need to do some post-installation configuration in order to make sure that everything will work properly.

Installing emulator system images

You need to install a system image for every Android SDK platform installed in case you want to run an emulator with this SDK platform as a target.

To do so, just follow these simple steps:

1. Go to the installation directory that you selected while installing TADP.

2. Open the SDK folder; in this case, it is `android-sdk-windows`.

3. Run the **SDK Manager**.

4. For every installed Android *X.X*, select a system image for the emulator, such as **ARM EABI V7a System Image**:

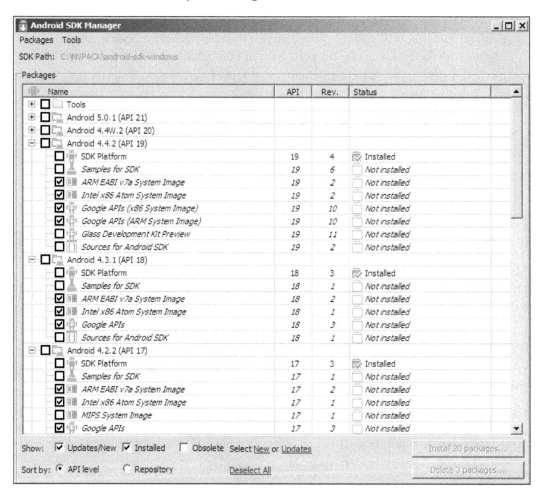

5. Click **Install packages**.
6. Read and accept the license agreement for the selected components.
7. Click **Install**.

Now, you can test your applications on an emulator of any of the installed targets.

Configuring Eclipse to work with NDK

You also need to configure Eclipse to run with NDK so that you can build your native apps directly from Eclipse:

1. Launch Eclipse from the installation directory that you specified earlier.
2. Open **Window | Preferences**.
3. In the pane on the left-hand side, open **Android Tree**.
4. Select the tree node labeled **NDK**.
5. In the right pane, click **Browse** and select the **NDK** directory; you will find it under the installation directory.
6. Click **OK**.

NDK verification

As the OpenCV libraries are written in C/C++, the first step to verify that your environment is working is to make sure that you are able to run Android applications that use native code.

1. Launch Eclipse.
2. From the **NDK** installation directory—in my case, `C:\NVPACK\android-ndk-r10c\`—import the `hello-jni` sample project from the `samples` folder as if you are importing any other Android project.
3. Right-click on the `HelloJni` project.
4. In the context menu, choose **Android Tools | Add Native Support**.
5. Make sure that the library name is set to `hello-jni`; it should be named this by default.
6. Start the emulator with the target of your choice.
7. Right click on the `hello-jni` project in the project explorer. In the context menu, choose **Run as | Android application**.

In your console output, there should be a list of `.so` files; these are the native shared libraries that NDK has built using **Application Binary Interface** (**ABI**), which defines exactly how your machine code should look.

Android NDK supports different architectures. By default, your `.so` will be built for ARM EABI in addition to MIPS and x86 if you specify so in the `application.mk` file. We will discuss this subject later in this chapter.

If everything runs smoothly, your emulator should have an app running as follows:

This application is very simple and a good checkpoint to verify that you are able to invoke native code from your Android application.

Basically, what you see on the emulator screen is a string returned from the native code and displayed by the Android framework in a text view.

Installing the OpenCV and Android development environment manually

To choose to manually install OpenCV and the Android development environment, you probably have the following installed components on your machine:

- Java SE Development Kit 6
- Android Studio
- Android SDK
- Eclipse IDE
- ADT and CDT plugin for Eclipse
- Android NDK
- OpenCV4Android SDK

You could go through the manual installation steps to make sure that you have all the needed components in order to start developing Android applications with OpenCV is ready and properly configured.

Java SE Development Kit 6

You can download the JDK installer for your OS from `http://www.oracle.com/technetwork/java/javase/downloads/index.html`.

Android Studio

Another very good option to work with is the Android Studio. You can download the Android Studio from `http://developer.android.com/sdk/index.html`. Note that Android Studio comes bundled with Android SDK, so you don't need to install it if you go with this option. Additionally, you can skip the Eclipse and ADT installation and note that starting from Android Studio 1.3; you will find built-in support for NDK as well.

Android SDK

To download and install Android SDK, follow these steps:

1. Go to `http://developer.android.com/sdk/index.html`.
2. Scroll down to the **SDK Tools Only** section and click on the `.exe` file of Windows installer link.

3. After you have read and accepted the terms and conditions, click the download button.

4. Save the installer on your disk and click on the `.exe` file to start the installer and then follow the onscreen instructions.

5. Keep a note of the SDK directory to refer to it later from the command line.

6. Once the installation is done, **Android SDK Manager** will start.

7. Select to install **Android SDK Tools**, revision 20 or newer.

8. For the SDK platform, Android, select **Android 3.0 (API 11)** or higher. In my case, I used **API 15** and you are recommended to do so.

9. Read and accept the license agreement, then click **Install**.

Eclipse IDE

For OpenCV 2.4.*x*, it is recommended to have Eclipse 3.7 (Indigo) or Eclipse 4.2 (Juno); you can download your selected version from Eclipse's official website at `http://www.eclipse.org/downloads/`.

ADT and CDT plugins for Eclipse

Assuming that you have already downloaded Eclipse, you can follow these steps to download the **Android Developer Tools (ADT)** and **C/C++ Development Tool (CDT)** plugins:

1. Launch Eclipse and then navigate to **Help | Install New Software**.

2. Click the **Add** button in the top corner to the right.

3. In the **Add Repository** dialog, write `ADT Plug-in` in the **Name** field and copy and paste this URL, `https://dl-ssl.google.com/android/eclipse/`, in the **Location** field.

4. Click **OK**.

5. Check the **Developer Tools** checkbox.

6. Click **Next**.

7. A list of the tools to be downloaded will be shown in the next window. Just make sure that it includes the native support tools (CDT) and click **Next**.

8. Read and accept the license agreement and click **Finish**.

9. Once the installation is complete, you will need to restart Eclipse.

Android NDK

In order to develop for Android in C++, you will need to install Android NDK.

 Android NDK is not meant to be used in all situations. As a developer, you need to balance between the performance gains that come with using a native API and the introduced complexity.

In our case, as the OpenCV libraries are written in C/C++, we might have to use NDK. However, using NDK shouldn't be just because the programmer prefers to write in C/C++.

Downloading Android NDK

You can download Android NDK by following these steps:

1. Go to the **Android NDK** home page, http://developer.android.com/tools/sdk/ndk/index.html.

2. In the **Downloads** section, select the version corresponding to your operating system. In my case, it is **Windows 64-bit**.

3. Read and agree with the terms and conditions.

4. Click the **Download** button.

Installing and configuring Android NDK

Once the download has finished, you will need to follow these steps to configure NDK:

1. Navigate to the **NDK** download folder.

2. Double-click on the downloaded file to extract it.

3. Rename and move the extracted folder; I'll refer to the ndk folder as <ndk_home>. Now you are ready to use NDK to build your projects.

4. If you prefer to build from the command line, you will need to add the <ndk_home> folder (in my case, C:/android/android-ndk-r10d) to your **PATH** environment variable. For Windows, open CMD. Enter the following command and replace the ndk directory with yours:

   ```
   set PATH=%PATH%;c:/android/android-ndk-r10d
   ```

5. To check that NDK is configured properly, go to the directory that contains your project. For simplicity, you can test on the hello-jni sample project. You can find it under <ndk_home>/samples/.

6. Change the directory by executing the command `cd <your_project_ directory>/`. Run the following command:

   ndk-build

7. As depicted in the console output, the files with the `.so` extension are the compiled version of the C/C++ source code used in this project:

```
C:\windows\system32\cmd.exe                                                          _|□|x|
C:\android\android-ndk-r10d\samples\hello-jni>ndk-build
Android NDK: WARNING: APP_PLATFORM android-15 is larger than android:minSdkVersion 3 in ./AndroidManifest.xml
[arm64-v8a] Gdbserver       : [aarch64-linux-android-4.9] libs/arm64-v8a/gdbserver
[arm64-v8a] Gdbsetup        : libs/arm64-v8a/gdb.setup
[x86_64] Gdbserver          : [x86_64-4.9] libs/x86_64/gdbserver
[x86_64] Gdbsetup           : libs/x86_64/gdb.setup
[mips64] Gdbserver          : [mips64el-linux-android-4.9] libs/mips64/gdbserver
[mips64] Gdbsetup           : libs/mips64/gdb.setup
[armeabi-v7a] Gdbserver     : [arm-linux-androideabi-4.6] libs/armeabi-v7a/gdbserver
[armeabi-v7a] Gdbsetup      : libs/armeabi-v7a/gdb.setup
[armeabi] Gdbserver         : [arm-linux-androideabi-4.6] libs/armeabi/gdbserver
[armeabi] Gdbsetup          : libs/armeabi/gdb.setup
[x86] Gdbserver             : [x86-4.6] libs/x86/gdbserver
[x86] Gdbsetup              : libs/x86/gdb.setup
[mips] Gdbserver            : [mipsel-linux-android-4.6] libs/mips/gdbserver
[mips] Gdbsetup             : libs/mips/gdb.setup
[arm64-v8a] Install         : libhello-jni.so => libs/arm64-v8a/libhello-jni.so
[x86_64] Install            : libhello-jni.so => libs/x86_64/libhello-jni.so
[mips64] Install            : libhello-jni.so => libs/mips64/libhello-jni.so
[armeabi-v7a] Install       : libhello-jni.so => libs/armeabi-v7a/libhello-jni.so
[armeabi] Install           : libhello-jni.so => libs/armeabi/libhello-jni.so
[x86] Install               : libhello-jni.so => libs/x86/libhello-jni.so
[mips] Install              : libhello-jni.so => libs/mips/libhello-jni.so

C:\android\android-ndk-r10d\samples\hello-jni>
```

Building native code using Eclipse

If you prefer to build from Eclipse, which is more convenient, you will need to tell Eclipse where to find NDK so that you can build your apps:

1. Launch Eclipse and open **Window** | **Preferences**.

2. In the left-hand side pane, open the **Android** tree.

3. Select the **NDK** tree node and in the right-hand side pane, click **Browse** and select the <ndk_home> directory.

4. Click **OK**.

5. Import the `hello-jni` sample project from <ndk_home>/samples/ as an Android project.

6. Open the Project Explorer and right-click on the `hello-jni` project.

7. In the context menu, navigate to **Android Tools** | **Add Native Support** to convert this project to a C++ project.

8. Accept the default library name and click **Finish**.

9. Build the application.

In the console, you will see a list of .so files, which are the compiled C++ part of this project. Still, if you open any C/C++ file from the imported project, you will see many highlighted errors. You just need to do some extra steps related to the CDT plugin:

1. Navigate to **Project | Properties**. In the left-hand side pane, expand the **C/C++ General** node.

2. Select **Paths and Symbols**.

3. In the right-hand side pane, select the **Includes** tab.

4. Click **Add** and then **File system** to add the following paths:

   ° If you installed NDK r8 or prior:

   ```
   <ndk_home>/platforms/android-9/arch-arm/usr/include<ndk_
   home>/sources/cxx-stl/gnu-libstdc++/include<ndk_home>/
   sources/cxx-stl/gnu-libstdc++/libs/armeabi-v7a/include
   ```

   ° If you installed NDK r8b or later:

   ```
   <ndk_home> /platforms/android-9/arch-arm/usr/include
   ```

   ```
   <ndk_home>/sources/cxx-stl/gnu-libstdc++/4.6/include
   ```

   ```
   <ndk_home> /sources/cxx-stl/gnu-libstdc++/4.6/libs/
   armeabi-v7a/include
   ```

5. Click **OK**. Eclipse will rebuild the project and all the syntax errors should be cleared from Eclipse.

6. Now, you can build the project to package both the Java and native code in one APK. To install the application on the emulator of your choice, use the menu item, **Run | Run As | Android Application**.

OpenCV4Android SDK

To be able to use the OpenCV collection of native (C/C++) libraries on your Android device, you need to install OpenCV4Android SDK, which is a part of OpenCV to run on the Android operating system.

1. First, go to the OpenCV download page, http://sourceforge.net/projects/opencvlibrary/files/opencv-android/.

2. Download the latest available version, which, at the time this book is being written, was **2.4.10**.

3. Extract the compressed file to a convenient path, for example, C:\opencv\.

[It is highly recommended to use paths with no spaces to avoid any problems with `ndk-build`.]

Understanding how NDK works

Whether you had a clean installation using TADP or followed the manual setup steps, at this stage you should have all the needed components to develop vision-aware Android applications.

Before we move forward to our first example, let's first elaborate on how NDK works. It's always a good idea to familiarize yourself with the basics of Android NDK and be comfortable using it as it will be a cornerstone to our development of Android applications using OpenCV.

An overview of NDK

If you decided to compile the native part of your Android application using the command prompt, you must have used the `ndk-build` tool. The `ndk-build` tool is actually a script that launches different build scripts that are responsible for the following:

- It automatically searches your project to decide on what to build
- Once the search is done, the scripts start generating binaries and managing dependencies
- It copies the generated binaries to your project path

Besides the `ndk-build` tool, there are a few other main components that you should be familiar with, including the following:

- **Java and native calls**: Android applications are written in Java, and once the source code is compiled, it is transformed to bytecode so that the Android OS runs under the **Dalvik** or **Android Runtime** (**ART**) virtual machine.

[Note that the applications that execute the native code are tested only on a Dalvik virtual machine.]

When you are using methods implemented in native code, you should use the `native` keyword.

For example, you could declare a function that multiplies two numbers and instructs the compiler that it is a native library:

```
public native double mul(double x, double y);
```

- **Native shared libraries**: NDK builds these libraries with an extension, `.so`. As the name suggests, these libraries are shared and linked in runtime.

- **Native static libraries**: NDK also builds these libraries with an extension, `.a`; these kind of libraries are actually linked at the compile time.

- **Java Native Interface (JNI)**: As you write your Android application in Java, you need a way to channel your calls to the native libraries written in C/C++ and that's where the JNI comes in handy.

- **Application Binary Interface (ABI)**: It is the interface that defines how your application machine code should look as you can run your application on different machine architectures. By default, NDK builds your code for ARM EABI; however, you can also select it to be built for MIPS or x86.

- **Android.mk**: Think of this file as a Maven build script or better, a make file, which instructs the `ndk-build` script about the definitions of the module and its name, the source files that you need to compile, and also the libraries that you need to link. It is very important to understand how to use this file and we will come back to it later for more details.

- **Application.mk**: It is optional to create this file and it is used to list the modules that your application requires. This information can include ABIs to generate machine code for a specific target architecture, toolchains, and standard libraries.

With these components in mind, you can summarize the general flow of developing native applications for Android as follows:

1. Decide which parts will be written in Java and which parts will be written in native C/C++.

2. Create an Android application in Eclipse.

3. Create an `Android.mk` file to define your module, list the native source code files to be compiled, and enumerate the linked libraries.

4. Create `Application.mk`; this is optional.

5. Copy your `Anrdoid.mk` file under the `jni` folder in your project path.

6. Build the project using Eclipse. As we linked Eclipse to the installed NDK, the `ndk-build` tool will compile the `.so`, `.a` libraries, your Java code will be compiled to the `.dex` files, and everything will be packaged in one single APK file and ready to be installed.

A simple example of NDK

As you will be developing Android applications with native support, you will need to be familiar with the general structure of a typical Android application using NDK.

Usually, your Android application has the following folder structure. The project `root` folder has the following subdirectories:

- `jni/`
- `libs/`
- `res/`
- `src/`
- `AndroidManifest.xml`
- `project.properties`

Here, the NDK-related folders are as follows:

- The `jni` folder will contain the native part of your application. In other words, this is the C/C++ source code with the NDK build scripts such as `Android.mk` and `Application.mk`, which are needed to build the native libraries.

- The `libs` folder will contain the native libraries after a successful build.

 The NDK build system requires both the `AndroidManifest.xml` and `project.properties` files to compile the native part of your application. So, if any of these files are missing, you will need to compile your Java code first before compiling the C/C++ code.

Android.mk

In this section, I'll describe the syntax of the `Android.mk` build file. As mentioned before, `Android.mk` is actually a GNU makefile fragment that the build system parses to know what to build in your project. The syntax of the file allows you to define modules. A module is one of the following:

- A static library
- A shared library
- A standalone executable

You already used `ndk-build` to build the `hello-jni` project, so let's take a look at the contents of this project `Android.mk` file:

```
LOCAL_PATH := $(call my-dir)
include $(CLEAR_VARS)

LOCAL_MODULE     := hello-jni
LOCAL_SRC_FILES := hello-jni.c

include $(BUILD_SHARED_LIBRARY)
```

Now, let's go through these lines one by one:

* `LOCAL_PATH := $(call my-dir)`: Here, the script defines a variable called `LOCAL_PATH` and sets its value by calling the `my-dir` function, which returns the current working directory.

* `include $(CLEAR_VARS)`: In this line, the script includes another GNU makefile called `CLEAR_VARS` to clear all the local variables — variables starting with `Local_xxx` with the exception of `LOCAL_PATH`. This is needed because the build files are parsed in a single-make execution context where all the variables are declared as global.

* `LOCAL_MODULE     := hello-jni`: Here, the script defines a module called `hello-jni`. The `LOCAL_MODULE` variable must be defined and unique to identify each module in `Android.mk`.

 The build system will add the `lib` prefix and `.so` suffix to your defined modules. In the example case, the generated library will be named `libhello-jni.so`.

* `LOCAL_SRC_FILES := hello-jni.c`: As the name suggests, you will list all the source files that you need be built and assembled in one module.

 You only list the source files and not the header files; it is the responsibility of the build system to compute the dependency for you.

* `include $(BUILD_SHARED_LIBRARY)`: Here we are including another GNU makefile, which will collect all the information that you defined after the last `include` command and decide what to build and how to build your module.

Building your first Android project with OpenCV

With the development environment up and running and having the proper NDK background, I can start assembling the big picture on how you can use the OpenCV libraries in your Android application.

OpenCV for Android supports access to its functions through its native API and also its Java wrappers API. In the case of a native API, you will define your native library using Android NDK and include the OpenCV libraries that you are using. Then, you will call your native library from the Java code using **Java Native Interface (JNI)**.

The other option is to use the OpenCV Java wrappers directly in your Java code using the usual Java imports. What will happen is that the Java wrappers will channel your calls to the native OpenCV libraries using JNI.

Of course, it is up to you to choose which style to go with; however, you should understand that using native calls could result in less JNI overhead but require more programming effort. On the other hand, using Java wrappers could cause more JNI overhead with less programming effort.

 Consider this scenario: you are processing a video frame or still image and in your algorithm, you will call several OpenCV functions. In this case, it is better to write one native library that calls all these functions. In your Android application, you can access this native library using only one JNI call.

HelloVisionWorld Android application

We will build our first Android application to grab preview frames from the camera in real time and display the preview on a fullscreen using OpenCV's Java camera API.

Creating a project in Eclipse

Following are the steps to create a project in Eclipse:

1. Launch Eclipse and create a new workspace.
2. Create a new Android project and name your application **HelloVisionWorld**.
3. Set the **Minimum SDK** version. To build with OpenCV4Android SDK, the minimum SDK version is 11; however, it is highly recommended to use **API 15** or higher. In my case, I used **API 15**.
4. Select **Target SDK**. In my case, I set it to **API 19**. Click **Next**.

5. Allow Eclipse to create **New Blank Activity** and name it
   `HelloVisionActivity` with a layout named `activity_hello_vision`.

6. Import the `OpenCV` library project to your workspace. Navigate to **File |
   Import | Existing Android Code Into Workspace**.

7. Select the `root` directory of OpenCV4Android SDK. **Deselect All** the sample
   projects and select only `OpenCV Library` and click `Finish`:

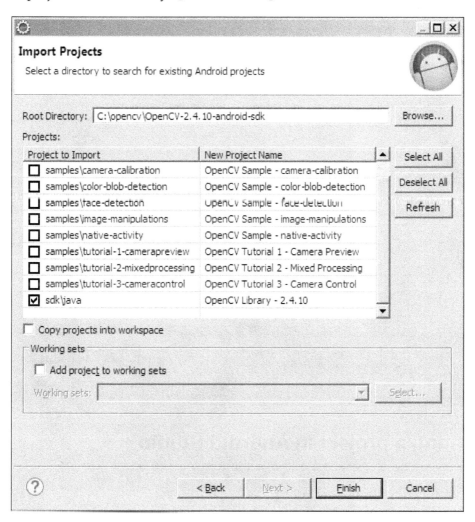

8. Reference the OpenCV library from your **Android** project. Click **Project | Properties**. Select the **Android** tree node from the left-hand side pane and in the right-hand side pane, click **Add** in the **Library** section and then **OK**:

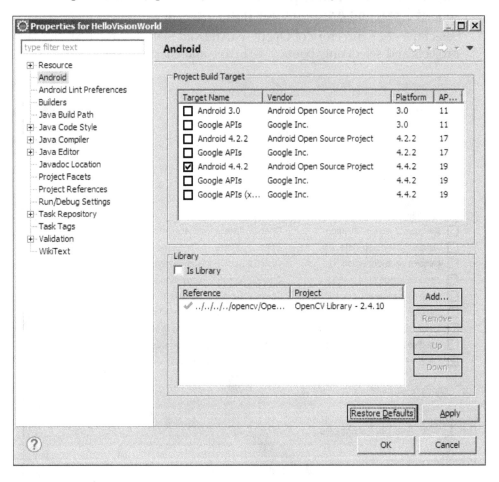

Creating a project in Android Studio

Following are the steps to create a project in Android Studio:

1. Launch **Android Studio**.

2. Create a new **Android Studio** project and name it HelloVisionWorld with **Company Domain** set to app0.com.

3. Choose **Minimum SDK**. To build with OpenCV4Android SDK, the **Minimum SDK** version is **11**.

4. Create a blank activity and name it HelloVisionActivity.

5. To add OpenCV as a dependency to your project, navigate to **File | New | Import Module** and **<OpenCV4Android_Directoy>\sdk\java**. Then, click **OK**. At this point, you may face some issues depending on the components installed from Android SDK. Android Studio will propose quick-fix links to solve such errors and it should be a straightforward fix.

6. Right-click on your newly created application in the project view and choose **Open Module Settings** or press *F4*.

7. In the **Dependencies** tab, press the **+** button and select **Module Dependency**.

8. Choose the OpenCV library and press **Add**. Now, you should be able to import the OpenCV classes to your project.

Moving forward, you should be able to follow the steps regardless of your choice of an IDE:

1. Open the layout file and edit it to match the following code. We added the OpenCV namespace and defined a Java camera view layout:

```
<RelativeLayout xmlns:android="http://schemas.android.com/apk/res/
android"
    xmlns:tools="http://schemas.android.com/tools"
    xmlns:opencv="http://schemas.android.com/apk/res-auto"
    android:layout_width="match_parent"
    android:layout_height="match_parent"
    android:paddingBottom="@dimen/activity_vertical_margin"
    android:paddingLeft="@dimen/activity_horizontal_margin"
    android:paddingRight="@dimen/activity_horizontal_margin"
    android:paddingTop="@dimen/activity_vertical_margin"
    tools:context="com.example.hellovisionworld.
HelloVisionActivity" >
    <org.opencv.android.JavaCameraView
        android:layout_width="fill_parent"
        android:layout_height="fill_parent"
        android:visibility="gone"
        android:id="@+id/HelloVisionView"
        opencv:show_fps="true"
        opencv:camera_id="any" />
</RelativeLayout>
```

Downloading the example code

You can download the example code files for all the Packt books that you have purchased from your account at http://www.packtpub.com. If you purchased this book elsewhere, you can visit http://www.packtpub.com/support and register in order to have the files e-mailed to you directly.

2. As we will be using the device camera, we need to set some permissions in the `AndroidManifest` file:

```
</application>

<uses-permission android:name="android.permission.CAMERA"/>

<uses-feature android:name="android.hardware.camera"
    android:required="false"/>
<uses-feature android:name="android.hardware.camera.autofocus"
    android:required="false"/>
<uses-feature android:name="android.hardware.camera.front"
    android:required="false"/>
<uses-feature
    android:name="android.hardware.camera.front.autofocus"
    android:required="false"/>
```

3. Hide the title and system buttons in the `AndroidManifest` file:

```
<application
    android:icon="@drawable/icon"
    android:label="@string/app_name"
    android:theme="@android:style/Theme.NoTitleBar.Fullscreen" >
```

4. We need to initialize the OpenCV library in the created activity. To do so, we use asynchronous initialization using the OpenCV Manager service to access the OpenCV libraries externally installed in the target system. First, we need to install the OpenCV Manager on the emulator that we will use. To do so, use the `adb install` command in the command prompt:

```
adb install <OpenCV4Android SDK_Home>\apk\OpenCV_2.4.X_
Manager_2.X_<platform>.apk
```

Replace `<OpenCV4Android SDK_Home>` with your OpenCV installation folder and `X` in the `apk` name with the available versions in your `apk` folder.

For `<platform>`, use the following table to choose which platform to install according to the system image that is installed on your emulator:

Hardware platform	Package name
armeabi-v7a (ARMv7-A + NEON)	OpenCV_2.4.X_Manager_2.X_armv7a-neon.apk
armeabi (ARMv5, ARMv6)	OpenCV_2.4.X_Manager_2.X_armeabi.apk
Intel x86	OpenCV_2.4.X_Manager_2.X_x86.apk
MIPS	OpenCV_2.4.X_Manager_2.X_mips.apk

When you are testing your application on a real device, a message will be displayed asking you to download the OpenCV manager from Google Play, so click **Yes** and check which version of OpenCV it supports so that you can load it through asynchronous initialization.

5. In `Activity`, define the following and fix the imports accordingly:

```
//A Tag to filter the log messages
private static final String  TAG = "Example::HelloVisionWorld::Act
ivity";


//A class used to implement the interaction between OpenCV and the
//device camera.
private CameraBridgeViewBase mOpenCvCameraView;


//This is the callback object used when we initialize the OpenCV
//library asynchronously
private BaseLoaderCallback mLoaderCallback = new
BaseLoaderCallback(this) {

    @Override
        //This is the callback method called once the OpenCV //
manager is connected
    public void onManagerConnected(int status) {
        switch (status) {
  //Once the OpenCV manager is successfully connected we
    can enable the camera interaction with the defined
    OpenCV camera view
        case LoaderCallbackInterface.SUCCESS:
          {
            Log.i(TAG, "OpenCV loaded successfully");
            mOpenCvCameraView.enableView();
          } break;
          default:
            {
              super.onManagerConnected(status);
            } break;
      }
    }
};
```

6. Update the `onResume` activity callback method to load the OpenCV library and fix the imports accordingly:

```
@Override
public void onResume(){

    super.onResume();

    //Call the async initialization and pass the callback object we
    //created later, and chose which version of OpenCV library to
    //load. Just make sure that the OpenCV manager you installed
    //supports the version you are trying to load.
      OpenCVLoader.initAsync(OpenCVLoader.OPENCV_VERSION_2_4_10,
        this, mLoaderCallback);
}
```

7. Your activity needs to implement `CvCameraViewListener2` to be able to receive camera frames from the OpenCV camera view:

```
public class HelloVisionActivity extends
    Activity implements CvCameraViewListener2
```

8. Fix the imports error accordingly and also insert the unimplemented methods in your activity.

9. In the `onCreate` activity callback method, we need to set the OpenCV camera view as visible and register your activity as the callback object that will handle the camera frames:

```
@Override
protected void onCreate(Bundle savedInstanceState) {
    Log.i(TAG, "called onCreate");

    super.onCreate(savedInstanceState);
      getWindow().addFlags
        (WindowManager.LayoutParams.FLAG_KEEP_SCREEN_ON);
    setContentView(R.layout.activity_hello_vision);

    mOpenCvCameraView = (CameraBridgeViewBase)
      findViewById(R.id.HelloVisionView);

    //Set the view as visible
    mOpenCvCameraView.setVisibility(SurfaceView.VISIBLE);

    //Register your activity as the callback object to handle
      //camera frames
    mOpenCvCameraView.setCvCameraViewListener(this);
}
```

10. The last step is to receive the camera frames. In order to do so, change the implementation of the `onCameraFrame` callback method:

```
public Mat onCameraFrame(CvCameraViewFrame inputFrame) {

    //We're returning the colored frame as is to be rendered on
      //thescreen.
    return inputFrame.rgba();
}
```

11. Now you're ready to build and install your application on the emulator or on a real device.

12. This is the application running on an emulated camera:

Summary

By now you should have developed and tested your first vision-aware Android application. In this chapter, you've learned how to set up an Android development environment with OpenCV using TADP or going through the manual scenario to update an existing one.

Moreover, you've learned the basics of NDK and how it works. Finally, you've seen how to capture camera frames using the OpenCV camera view and display the frames on the device screen. This example will be our building block to implement more interesting ideas.

2
App 1 - Building Your Own Darkroom

In this chapter, you will learn about how images are stored and represented in OpenCV and how to utilize this representation to implement interesting algorithms that will enhance how your images look.

We will first explain the digital image representation and different color spaces to explore the important Mat class in OpenCV.

Then, we will go through the steps to load an image from your phone gallery and display it on your device screen regardless of the image resolution.

Finally, you will learn about the image histograms and how to calculate and use them to enhance your images, whether they are black and white or colored.

We will cover the following topics in this chapter:

- Digital images
- Processing the images stored on your phone
- Calculating an image histogram
- Enhancing the image contrast

Digital images

Images can be found around us wherever we look; so it is very important to understand how images are represented and how the images' colors are mapped if we want to understand, process, and analyze these images automatically.

Color spaces

We live in a continuous world, so to capture a scene in a discreet digital sensor, a discrete spatial (layout) and intensity (color information) mapping has to happen in order to store the real-world data in a digital image.

The two-dimensional digital image, D(i,j), represents a sensor response value at the pixel indicated by the row number *i* and column number *j*, starting from the left upper corner as *i=j=0*.

To represent colors, a digital image usually contains one or more channels to store the intensity value (color) of each pixel. The most widely used color representation is a one-channel image, also known as a grayscale image, where every pixel is assigned a shade of gray depending on its intensity value: zero is black and the maximum intensity value is white.

If an unsigned character, taking values from 0 to 2^8-1, is used to represent the color depth information, then each pixel can store an intensity value from 0 (black) to 255 (white).

In addition to grayscale color mapping, there is also true color mapping where the color is represented by three channels instead of one and the pixel value becomes a tuple of three elements (Red, Green, and Blue). In this case, the color is represented as a linear combination of the three channels' values and the image is considered to be three two-dimensional planes.

 Sometimes, a fourth channel called **Alpha** is added and used to represent the color transparency. In this case, the image will be considered as four two-dimensional planes.

There is one more color space to consider that is more related to human understanding and perception of colors than the RGB representation. It is the **Hue, Saturation, and Value (HSV)** color space.

Each of the color dimensions can be understood as follows:

- **Hue (H)**: It is the color itself, Red, Blue, or Green.
- **Saturation (S)**: It measures how pure the color is; for example, is it a dull red or dark red? Think of it as how much white is blinded with the color.
- **Value (V)**: It is the brightness of the color, also known as luminance.

The last image type to consider is the binary image. It is a two-dimensional array of pixels; however, each pixel can store only the value of zero or one. This type or representation is important to the solving of vision problems such as edge detection.

Having a two-dimensional array of pixels or three two-dimensional planes to represent the images with each cell or pixel containing the intensity value of the color in case of an RGB color space or the Hue, Saturation, and Value in case of an HSV color space, reduces the image to a numerical matrix. As OpenCV's main focus is to process and manipulate images, the first thing that you will need to understand is how OpenCV stores and handles the images.

The Mat class

The most important and fundamental data structure that you will be using when developing vision-aware applications using OpenCV is the Mat class.

The Mat class represents an *n*-dimensional dense numerical single-channel or multichannel array. Basically, if you are using the Mat class to represent a grayscale image, then your Mat object will be a two-dimensional array (with one channel) storing the pixel intensity values. If you are using the Mat class to store a full color image, then the Mat object will be a two-dimensional array with three channels (one channel for Red intensities, one for Green, and one for Blue) and the same applies to the HSV color space.

As with any Java class, the Mat class has a list of constructors and, in most cases, the default constructor will be sufficient. However, in some other cases, you might want to initialize a Mat object with a specific size, type, and number of channels.

In this case, you can use the following constructor:

```
int numRow=5;
int numCol=5;
int type=org.opencv.core.CvType.CV_8UC1;
Mat myMatrix=newMat(numRow,numCol,type);
```

This constructor takes three integer parameters:

- int Rows: The number of the new matrix rows
- int Cols: The number of the new matrix columns
- int type: The new matrix type

In order to specify what type the Mat class is storing and how many channels there are, OpenCV provides you with a CvType class with `static int` fields with the following naming convention:

CV_(Data type size ["8" | "16" | "32" | "64"])(["S" | "U" | "F" , for signed, unsigned integers, or floating point numbers])(Number of channels["C1 | C2 | C3 | C4", for one, two, three, or four channels respectively])

For example, you specified the type parameter as `org.opencv.core.CvType.CV_8UC1`; this means that the matrix will hold 8-bit unsigned characters for color intensity with one channel. In other words, this matrix will store a grayscale image with intensities from 0 (black) to 255 (white).

Basic Mat operations

Besides understanding how digital images are represented in the OpenCV library, you will need to be familiar with some basic operations that you can perform on the Mat object.

The most fundamental operation that you can do is pixel-level access to retrieve the pixel value whether your color space is grayscale or full RGB. Assuming that you have the sample application from *Chapter 1*, *Getting Yourself Ready*, up and running, you can recall that in the `onCameraFrame()` callback method, we were retrieving the full color camera frame using the `inputFrame.rgba()` method.

With the camera frame, we can access the pixel value using the following code:

```
@Override
  public Mat onCameraFrame(CvCameraViewFrameinputFrame) {
    Mat cameraFram=inputFrame.rgba();
    double [] pixelValue=cameraFram.get(0, 0);
    double redChannelValue=pixelValue[0];
    double greenChannelValue=pixelValue[1];
    double blueChannelValue=pixelValue[2];
    Log.i(TAG, "red channel value: "+redChannelValue);
    Log.i(TAG, "green channel value: "+greenChannelValue);
    Log.i(TAG, "blue channel value: "+blueChannelValue);
    return inputFrame.rgba();
  }
```

Let's go through the important lines and the rest is actually straightforward:

```
double [] pixelValue=cameraFram.get(0, 0);
```

In this line, we are calling the `get(0,0)` function and passing it to the row and column index; in this case, it is the top left pixel.

Note that the `get()` method returns a double array because the Mat object can hold up to four channels.

In our case, it is a full color image, so each pixel will have three intensities for each of the Red (`r`), Green (`g`), and Blue (`b`) color channels in addition to one channel for the transparency, Alpha (`a`), hence the name of the method is `rgba()`.

You can access each channel intensity independently using the array index operator `[]` so, for the Red, Green, and Blue intensities, you use `0`, `1`, and `2`, respectively:

```
double redChannelValue=pixelValue[0];
double greenChannelValue=pixelValue[1];
double blueChannelValue=pixelValue[2];
```

The following table is a list of the basic `Mat` class operations that you will need to be familiar with:

Functionality	Code sample

To retrieve the number of channels	`Mat myImage; //declared and initialized`
	`int numberOfChannels=myImage.channels();`

To make a deep copy of a Mat object including the matrix data	`Mat newMat=existingMat.clone();`

To retrieve the number of matrix columns	**First method:**
	`Mat myImage; //declared and initialized`
	`int colsNum=myImage.cols();`
	Second method:
	`int colsNum=myImage.width();`
	Third method:
	`//And yes, it is a public instance variable.`
	`int colsNum=myImage.size().width;`

Functionality	Code sample

To retrieve the number of matrix rows	**First method:**
	
	```Mat myImage; //declared and initialized```
	```int rowsNum=myImage.rows();```
	
	Second method:
	
	```int rowsNum=myImage.height();```
	
	Thirst method:
	
	```//And yes, it is a public instance variable.```
	```int rowsNum=myImage.size().height;```

To retrieve the matrix element depth (the type of each individual channel):
 	
• CV_8U: 8-bit unsigned integers (0 to 255)
 	
• CV_8S: 8-bit signed integers (-128 to 127)
 	
• CV_16U: 16-bit unsigned integers (0 to 65,535)
 	
• CV_16S: 16-bit signed integers (-32,768 to 32,767)
 	
• CV_32S: 32-bit signed integers (-2,147,483,648 to 2,147,483,647)
 	
• CV_32F: 32-bit floating-point numbers
 	
• CV_64F: 64-bit floating-point numbers
	```Mat myImage; //declared and initialized```
	```int depth=myImage.depth()```

To retrieve the total number of matrix elements (number of pixels in an image)	```Mat myImage; //declared and initialized```
	```long numberOfPixels=myImage.total()```

Processing the images stored on your phone

In this section, you will learn how to load an image from your phone and apply some interesting image processing algorithms to it, such as contrast enhancing, smoothing (removing noise from your image), and applying some filters.

Loading an image to a Mat object

Let's get started by first creating a new Android project. As you've seen in the previous chapter, in order to start using the OpenCV algorithms, you will need to add the OpenCV library to your project:

1. Launch **Eclipse**.
2. Create a new Android project application; let's name it DarkRoom.
3. Choose the package name. In this example, I chose it to be com.example. chapter2.darkroom.
4. Set the minimum required SDK to be anything above **API 11 (Android 3.0)**. In my case, and it is highly recommended, I chose it to be **API 16 (Android 4.1)**. For the target SDK, you should choose **API 19** because there is an issue when loading the OpenCV library if you are using a target SDK higher than 19.
5. Click **Next**.
6. Let Eclipse create a blank activity for you and name it IODarkRoom.
7. Finish creating the project.
8. Import the OpenCV library project to your workspace file, **Menu | Import | Existing Android Code Into Workspace**.
9. Click **Browse** and go to your OpenCV installation home directory.
10. Select the OpenCV home directory and click **Ok**.
11. Deselect all the projects and select only the OpenCV library project.
12. Click **Finish**.
13. Now, you need to link your newly created Android project with the OpenCV library that you just imported so, on the new project, right-click **Properties**.
14. In the left pane, select the Android tree node and in the right pane, click **Add**.
15. Select the OpenCV library and click **Ok**.

UI definitions

In this project, you will load an image stored on your phone, convert it to a bitmap image, and display it in an image view.

Let's start by setting the layout of the application activity:

```
<LinearLayoutxmlns:android="http://schemas.android.com/apk/res/
android"
android:layout_width="fill_parent"
android:layout_height="fill_parent"
android:orientation="horizontal">
  <ImageView
  android:id="@+id/IODarkRoomImageView"
  android:layout_width="fill_parent"
  android:layout_height="fill_parent"
  android:src="@drawable/ic_launcher"
  android:layout_marginLeft="0dp"
  android:layout_marginTop="0dp"
  android:scaleType="fitXY"/>
</LinearLayout>
```

It is a simple linear layout with an image view. The next step is to set some needed permissions. Just in case you will be loading images from your SD card, you will need to set the corresponding permission so that Android allows your application to read and write from the external storage.

In your manifest file, add the following line:

```
<uses-permissionandroid:name=
   "android.permission.WRITE_EXTERNAL_STORAGE"/>
```

It is a write permission; however, your application is also implicitly granted a read permission as it is less restrictive.

Now, let's move on to the application and activity definition:

```
<application
android:allowBackup="true"
android:icon="@drawable/ic_launcher"
android:label="@string/app_name"
android:theme="@style/AppTheme">
  <activity
  android:name=".IODarkRoom"
  android:label="@string/app_name"
  android:screenOrientation="portrait">
    <intent-filter>
```

```
        <actionandroid:name="android.intent.action.MAIN"/>

        <categoryandroid:name="android.intent.category.LAUNCHER"/>
    </intent-filter>
  </activity>
</application>
```

It is a very straightforward definition; however, without a loss of generality, I restricted the orientation of the activity to be portrait, which means that your activity will not support the landscape mode. This will put the focus on image manipulation instead of handling different activity modes. However, I encourage you to extend this application to also support landscape orientation after digesting the content of this chapter as it will give you a good hands-on experience.

We will need a menu item for every action that we will support in the application. Our first action will be opening the gallery on your phone in order to select a specific image and for this, you will need to add the following menu item to the file:

```
res/menu/iodark_room.xml
<item
android:id="@+id/action_openGallary"
android:orderInCategory="100"
android:showAsAction="never"
android:title="@string/action_OpenGallary"/>
```

Add the corresponding string definition to res/values/strings.xml:

```
<stringname="action_OpenGallary">Open Gallary</string>
```

We are done with the UI definitions for this part of the application, so let's move on to the code behind it.

Reading an image using OpenCV

The first step is to load the OpenCV library asynchronously using the OpenCV manager service to reduce the memory footprint of your application. To do so, you will need to have this boilerplate code in every activity that will be using the OpenCV algorithms:

```
private BaseLoaderCallback mLoaderCallback =
newBaseLoaderCallback(this) {
  @Override
  public void onManagerConnected(int status) {
    switch (status) {
      case LoaderCallbackInterface.SUCCESS:
      {
```

```
            Log.i(TAG, "OpenCV loaded successfully");
        } break;
        default:
        {
            super.onManagerConnected(status);
        } break;
    }
  }
};


@Override
  public void onResume()
  {
    super.onResume();
    OpenCVLoader.initAsync(OpenCVLoader.OPENCV_VERSION_2_4_8,
      this, mLoaderCallback);
  }
```

The next step is to handle the user clicks on the menu item that we defined earlier:

```
private static final int SELECT_PICTURE = 1;
private String selectedImagePath;
@Override
  public boolean onOptionsItemSelected(MenuItem item) {
    // Handle action bar item clicks here. The action bar will
    // automatically handle clicks on the Home/Up button, so long
    // as you specify a parent activity in AndroidManifest.xml.
    int id = item.getItemId();
    if (id == R.id.action_openGallary) {
      Intent intent = newIntent();
      intent.setType("image/*");
      intent.setAction(Intent.ACTION_GET_CONTENT);
      startActivityForResult(Intent.createChooser(intent,
        "Select Picture"), SELECT_PICTURE);
      return true;
    }
    return super.onOptionsItemSelected(item);
  }
```

Once the user selects an image to load from the gallery, we execute the loading and display it in the activity result callback method:

```
public void onActivityResult(int requestCode, int resultCode,
  Intent data) {
  if (resultCode == RESULT_OK) {
    if (requestCode == SELECT_PICTURE) {
```

```
        Uri selectedImageUri = data.getData();
        selectedImagePath = getPath(selectedImageUri);
        Log.i(TAG, "selectedImagePath: " + selectedImagePath);
        loadImage(selectedImagePath);
        displayImage(sampledImage);
      }
    }
  }
```

After you make sure that the opened activity returned the needed result—in this case, it is the image URI—we call the helper method, getPath(), to retrieve the image path in the format that is needed to load the image using OpenCV:

```
private String getPath(Uri uri) {
  // just some safety built in
  if(uri == null ) {
    return null;
  }
  // try to retrieve the image from the media store first
  // this will only work for images selected from gallery
  String[] projection = { MediaStore.Images.Media.DATA };
  Cursor cursor = getContentResolver().query(uri, projection,
    null, null, null);
  if(cursor != null ){
    int column_index = cursor.getColumnIndexOrThrow(
      MediaStore.Images.Media.DATA);
    cursor.moveToFirst();
    return cursor.getString(column_index);
  }
  return uri.getPath();
}
```

Once we have the path ready, we call the loadImage() method:

```
private void loadImage(String path)
{
  originalImage = Highgui.imread(path);
  Mat rgbImage=new Mat();

  Imgproc.cvtColor(originalImage, rgbImage,
    Imgproc.COLOR_BGR2RGB);

  Display display = getWindowManager().getDefaultDisplay();
  //This is "android graphics Point" class
  Point size = new Point();
```

```
       display.getSize(size);

       int width = size.x;
       int height = size.y;
       sampledImage=new Mat();

       double downSampleRatio= calculateSubSampleSize(
         rgbImage,width,height);

       Imgproc.resize(rgbImage, sampledImage, new Size(),
         downSampleRatio,downSampleRatio,Imgproc.INTER_AREA);

       try {
         ExifInterface exif = new ExifInterface(selectedImagePath);
         int orientation = exif.getAttributeInt(
           ExifInterface.TAG_ORIENTATION, 1);

         switch (orientation)
         {
           case ExifInterface.ORIENTATION_ROTATE_90:
             //get the mirrored image
             sampledImage=sampledImage.t();
             //flip on the y-axis
             Core.flip(sampledImage, sampledImage, 1);
             break;
           case ExifInterface.ORIENTATION_ROTATE_270:
             //get up side down image
             sampledImage=sampledImage.t();
             //Flip on the x-axis
             Core.flip(sampledImage, sampledImage, 0);
             break;
         }
       } catch (IOException e) {
         e.printStackTrace();
       }
     }
```

Let's go through the code step by step:

```
     originalImage = Highgui.imread(path);
```

This method reads an image from the given path and returns it. It is provided as a static member in the Highgui class.

If you are loading a colored image, it is very important to know the order of the color channels. In the case of `imread()`, the decoded image will have the channels stored in a B, G, R order.

Now, let us see the following snippet:

```
Mat rgbImage=new Mat();

Imgproc.cvtColor(originalImage, rgbImage, Imgproc.COLOR_BGR2RGB);
```

In order to load the image as an RGB bitmap, we first need to convert the decoded image from the color space B, G, R to the color space R, G, B.

First, we instantiate an empty Mat object, `rgbImage`, then we execute color space mapping using the `Imgproc.cvtColor()` method. The method takes three parameters: the source image, destination image, and mapping code. Luckily, OpenCV supports over 150 mappings and, in our case, we need the BGR to RGB mapping. Now, let us see the following snippet:

```
Display display = getWindowManager().getDefaultDisplay();
Point size = new Point();
display.getSize(size);

int width = size.x;
int height = size.y;
double downSampleRatio= calculateSubSampleSize(
  rgbImage,width,height);
```

It would be very wasteful and sometimes impossible to display the images in their original resolution due to memory constraints.

For example, if you captured an image with your phone's 8 megapixel camera, then the memory cost of the colored image, assuming 1 byte color depth, is $8 \times 3 (RGB) = 24\, megabyte$.

To overcome this issue, it is advisable to resize (downsample) the image to your phone's display resolution. To do so, we first retrieve the phone's display resolution and then calculate the downsample ratio using the `calculateSubSampleSize()` helper method:

```
private static double calculateSubSampleSize(
  Mat srcImage, int reqWidth, int reqHeight) {
  // Raw height and width of image
  final int height = srcImage.height();
```

```
         final int width = srcImage.width();
         double inSampleSize = 1;

         if (height > reqHeight || width > reqWidth) {

           // Calculate ratios of requested height and width to the raw
           //height and width
           final double heightRatio = (double) reqHeight / (double) height;
           final double widthRatio = (double) reqWidth / (double) width;

           // Choose the smallest ratio as inSampleSize value, this will
           //guarantee final image with both dimensions larger than or
           //equal to the requested height and width.
           inSampleSize = heightRatio<widthRatio ?
             heightRatio :widthRatio;
         }
         return inSampleSize;
     }
```

The `calculateSubSampleSize()` method takes three arguments: the source image, required width, and required height, then computes the downsample ratio. Now, let us see the following snippet:

```
sampledImage=new Mat();
Imgproc.resize(rgbImage, sampledImage, new Size(),
  downSampleRatio,downSampleRatio,Imgproc.INTER_AREA);
```

Now, we are ready to resize the loaded image to fit on the device screen. First, we create an empty Mat object, `sampledImage`, to hold the resized image. Then, we call `Imgproc.resize()` passing to it:

- The source Mat object, the one that we need to resize

- The destination Mat object

- The size of the new image; in our case, a new empty `Size` object as we will send the downsample ratio instead

- A double for the downsample ratio in the X direction (for the width)

- A double for the downsample ratio in the Y direction (for the height)

- An integer for the interpolation method; the default value is INTER_LINEAR, which corresponds to the linear interpolation

Interpolation is needed here because we will change the size of an image (upsize or downsize) and we want the mapping from the source image to the destination image to be as smooth as possible.

Interpolation will decide what the value of the destination image pixel is when it falls between two pixels in the source image in case we are downsizing. It will also compute the value of the new pixels in the destination image, which doesn't have a corresponding pixel in the source image, in case we are upsizing.

In either case, OpenCV has several options to compute the value of such pixels. The default INTER_LINEAR method computes the destination pixel value by linearly weighing the 2-by-2 surrounding source pixels' values according to how close they are to the destination pixel. Alternatively, INTER_NEAREST takes the value of the destination pixel from its closest pixel in the source image. The INTER_AREA option virtually places the destination pixel over the source pixels and then averages the covered pixel values. Finally, we have the option of fitting a cubic spline between the 4-by-4 surrounding pixels in the source image and then reading off the corresponding destination value from the fitted spline; this is the result of choosing the INTER_CUBIC interpolation method.

To shrink an image, it will generally look best with the INTER_AREA interpolation, whereas to enlarge an image, it will generally look best with INTER_CUBIC (slow) or INTER_LINEAR (faster, but still looks OK).

```
try {
  ExifInterface exif = new ExifInterface(selectedImagePath);
  int orientation = exif.getAttributeInt(
    ExifInterface.TAG_ORIENTATION, 1);

  switch (orientation)
  {
    case ExifInterface.ORIENTATION_ROTATE_90:
      //get the mirrored image
      sampledImage=sampledImage.t();
      //flip on the y-axis
      Core.flip(sampledImage, sampledImage, 1);
      break;
    case ExifInterface.ORIENTATION_ROTATE_270:
      //get upside down image
      sampledImage=sampledImage.t();
      //Flip on the x-axis
      Core.flip(sampledImage, sampledImage, 0);
      break;
  }
} catch (IOException e) {
  e.printStackTrace();
}
```

Now, we need to handle the image orientation and because the activity only works in the portrait mode, we will handle the images with a rotation of 90 or 270 degrees.

In the case of a 90 degree rotation, this means that you took the image with the phone in the portrait position; we rotate the image 90 degrees counterclockwise by calling the `t()` method in order to transpose the Mat object.

The result of the transpose is a mirrored version of the original image, so we need one more step to flip the image around the vertical axis by calling `Core.flip()` and passing it to the source image and destination image and calling a flip code to specify how to flip the image; `0` means flipping around the x axis, a positive value (for example, `1`) means flipping around the y axis, and a negative value (for example, `-1`) means flipping around both the axes.

For the 270 degree rotation case, this means that you took the picture with your phone upside down. We follow the same algorithm, transpose the image and then flip it. Yet, after we transpose the image, it will be a mirrored version around the horizontal direction, thus we call `Core.flip()` with the `0` flip code.

Now, we are ready to display the image using the image view component:

```
private void displayImage(Mat image)
{
  // create a bitMap
  Bitmap bitMap = Bitmap.createBitmap(image.cols(),
    image.rows(),Bitmap.Config.RGB_565);
  // convert to bitmap:
  Utils.matToBitmap(image, bitMap);

  // find the imageview and draw it!
  ImageView iv = (ImageView) findViewById(
    R.id.IODarkRoomImageView);
  iv.setImageBitmap(bitMap);
}
```

First, we create a bitmap object with the color channels' order matching the loaded image color channels' order, RGB. Then, we use `Utils.matToBitmap()` to convert a Mat object to a bitmap object. Finally, we set the image view bitmap with the newly created bitmap object.

Calculating an image histogram

We are one step closer to understanding the image content, and one of the fundamental image analysis techniques is calculating the image histogram.

What are histograms?

Histograms are plots used to give you an overall idea about the distribution of the intensity values of a given image. In the x axis, the plot will have values ranging from 0 to 255 depending on the image depth as explained earlier and the y axis will represent the number of occurrences of the corresponding intensity value.

Once you calculate and display the histogram of an image, you can easily gain some insights about the image contrast, intensity distribution, and so on. Actually, if you normalize the histogram, making it sum to one, you can treat the histogram as a probability density function and answer questions such as what is the probability of a given intensity value to occur on an image and the answer is simply the y axis reading at that intensity value. In the following figure, you can see that pixels with an intensity of 50 appears in the image on the left 5,000 times:

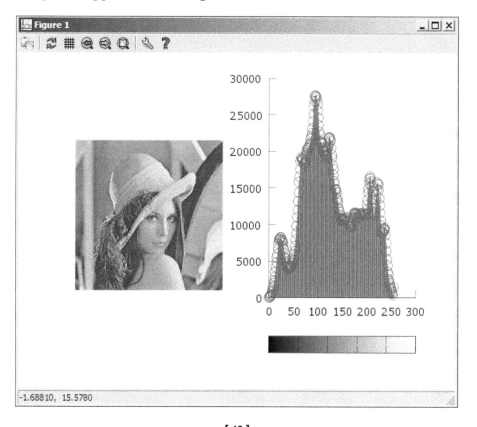

Understanding histogram components

Before we dive in and start calculating histograms, we need to understand some components and terminologies to calculate a histogram:

- **Histogram bins**: As explained earlier, the x axis of the histogram plot represents the intensity values that each pixel can store.

  For example, if you are displaying a histogram for the intensities from 0 to 255, you will need 256 bins to hold the number of occurrences for each intensity value. However, this is usually not the case as this is considered a very fine-grained histogram and the results may not be very informative.

  To fix this, you can divide the histogram into bins and every bin holds a range of intensities.

  For our example, from 0 to 255, we can have 25 bins and every bin will hold the value for ten consecutive intensity values, from 0 to 9, and from 10 to 19, and so on. Yet, if the histogram is still not very representative, you can decrease the number of bins in order to increase the range of intensity values in every bin.

- **Histogram dimensions**: In our case, the number of dimensions is one as we will be considering only the intensity value for each pixel for one channel in the case of a grayscale image or an individual color channel in the case of a full color image.

- **Histogram range**: This is the limit of values to be measured. In our example, we have intensities ranging from 0 to 255, so the range of values that we want to measure will be (0, 255), that is, all the intensities.

Now, we are ready to show how to calculate a histogram for an image using the OpenCV library.

UI definitions

We will continue to build on the same app that we started in the previous section. The change is to add one more menu item to the menu file in order to trigger the histogram calculation.

Go to the `res/menu/iodark_room.xml` file and open it to include the following menu item:

```
<item
android:id="@+id/action_Hist"
android:orderInCategory="101"
android:showAsAction="never"
android:title="@string/action_Hist">
</item>
```

This is it, in terms of UI changes.

Calculating an image histogram

In the IODarkRoom activity, we need to handle the user pressing the display histogram menu item.

Edit the onOptionesItemSelected() method as follows:

```
@Override
public boolean onOptionsItemSelected(MenuItem item) {
  // Handle action bar item clicks here. The action bar will
  // automatically handle clicks on the Home/Up button, so long
  // as you specify a parent activity in AndroidManifest.xml.
  int id = item.getItemId();
  if (id == R.id.action_openGallary) {
    Intent intent = newIntent();
    intent.setType("image/*");
    intent.setAction(Intent.ACTION_GET_CONTENT);
    startActivityForResult(Intent.createChooser(intent,
      "Select Picture"), SELECT_PICTURE);
    return true;
  }
  else if (id == R.id.action_Hist) {
    if(sampledImage==null)
    {
      Context context = getApplicationContext();
      CharSequence text = "You need to load an image first!";
      int duration = Toast.LENGTH_SHORT;

      Toast toast = Toast.makeText(context, text, duration);
      toast.show();
      return true;
    }
    Mat histImage=new Mat();
    sampledImage.copyTo(histImage);
    calcHist(histImage);
    displayImage(histImage);
    return true;
  }
  return super.onOptionsItemSelected(item);
}
```

Note that in case the display histogram menu item is pressed, we first check to see that the user already loaded an image and in case he didn't, we display a friendly message and then return it.

Now for the histogram part, which is as follows:

```
Mat histImage=new Mat();
sampledImage.copyTo(histImage);

calcHist(histImage);

displayImage(histImage);
return true;
```

We first make a copy of the downsized image that the user loaded; this is necessary as we will change the image to display the histogram, so we need to have a pristine copy. Once we have the copy, we call `calcHist()` and pass it to the new image:

```
private void calcHist(Mat image)
{
  int mHistSizeNum = 25;
  MatOfInt mHistSize = new MatOfInt(mHistSizeNum);
  Mat hist = new Mat();
  float []mBuff = new float[mHistSizeNum];
  MatOfFloat histogramRanges = new MatOfFloat(0f, 256f);
  Scalar mColorsRGB[] = new Scalar[] { new Scalar(200, 0, 0, 255),
    new Scalar(0, 200, 0, 255), new Scalar(0, 0, 200, 255) };
  org.opencv.core.PointmP1 = new org.opencv.core.Point();
  org.opencv.core.PointmP2 = new org.opencv.core.Point();

  int thikness = (int) (image.width() / (mHistSizeNum+10)/3);
  if(thikness> 3) thikness = 3;
  MatOfInt mChannels[] = new MatOfInt[] { new MatOfInt(0),
    new MatOfInt(1), new MatOfInt(2) };
  Size sizeRgba = image.size();
  int offset = (int) ((sizeRgba.width -
    (3*mHistSizeNum+30)*thikness));
  // RGB
  for(int c=0; c<3; c++) {
    Imgproc.calcHist(Arrays.asList(image), mChannels[c], new
      Mat(), hist, mHistSize, histogramRanges);
    Core.normalize(hist, hist, sizeRgba.height/2, 0,
      Core.NORM_INF);
    hist.get(0, 0, mBuff);
    for(int h=0; h<mHistSizeNum; h++) {
```

```
mP1.x = mP2.x = offset + (c * (mHistSizeNum + 10) + h) *
    thikness;
mP1.y = sizeRgba.height-1;
mP2.y = mP1.y - (int)mBuff[h];
Core.line(image, mP1, mP2, mColorsRGB[c], thikness);
    }
  }
}
```

The `calcHist()` method is divided into two parts.

The first part is related to configuring the histogram's look and defining the histogram components:

```
int mHistSizeNum = 25;
MatOfInt mHistSize = new MatOfInt(mHistSizeNum);
```

First, we define the number of histogram bins. In this case, our histogram will have 25 bins. Then, we initialize a `MatOfInt()` object, which is a subclass of the `Mat` class but only stores integers, with the number of histogram bins. The result of such an initialization is a `MatOfInt` object of the dimension, $1 \times 1 \times 1 (rows \times columns \times channels)$, holding the number 25.

 We need to initialize such an object because, according to the specification, the OpenCV calculate histogram method takes a Mat object holding the number of histogram bins.

Then, we initialize a new Mat object to hold the histogram value using the following command:

```
Mat hist = newMat();
```

This time, the Mat object will have the dimension, $1 \times 1 \times number\ of\ bins$:

```
float []mBuff = new float[mHistSizeNum];
```

Recall that in the beginning of this chapter, we accessed individual pixels in the image. Here, we will use the same technique to access the histogram bins' values and store them in an array of the float type. Here we are defining another histogram component, which is the histogram range:

```
MatOfFloat histogramRanges = new MatOfFloat(0f, 256f);
```

We use the `MatOfFloat()` class; it is a subclass of the `Mat` class and as the name suggests, it only holds floating point numbers.

The result of such an initialization will be a Mat object of the dimension, 2×1×1, holding the values 0 and 256, respectively:

```
Scalar mColorsRGB[] = new Scalar[] { new Scalar(200, 0, 0, 255),
    new Scalar(0, 200, 0, 255), new Scalar(0, 0, 200, 255) };
```

As we are creating a histogram of every channel, we will distinguish between every channel's histogram by plotting its lines with the corresponding channel color. We initialize an array of three `Scalar` objects, which is simply a double array of a length up to four, representing the three colors, Red, Green, and Blue. Initialize two points to draw a line for every histogram bin:

```
org.opencv.core.PointmP1 = new org.opencv.core.Point();
org.opencv.core.PointmP2 = new org.opencv.core.Point();
```

For every line that we draw for the histogram bin, we need to specify the line thickness:

```
int thikness = (int) (image.width() / (mHistSizeNum+10)/3);
if(thikness> 3) thikness = 3;
```

Initialize three `MatOfInt` objects with the values 0, 1, and 2 to index every image channel independently:

```
MatOfInt mChannels[] = new MatOfInt[] { new MatOfInt(0),
    new MatOfInt(1), new MatOfInt(2) };
```

Calculate the offset from which we will start drawing the histogram:

```
Size sizeRgba = image.size();
int offset = (int) ((sizeRgba.width -
    (3*mHistSizeNum+30)*thikness));
```

Let's move forward to part two where we calculate and plot the histogram:

```
// RGB
for(int c=0; c<3; c++) {
    Imgproc.calcHist(Arrays.asList(image), mChannels[c], new Mat(),
        hist, mHistSize, histogramRanges);

    Core.normalize(hist, hist, sizeRgba.height/2, 0, Core.NORM_INF);

    hist.get(0, 0, mBuff);

    for(int h=0; h<mHistSizeNum; h++) {
```

```
    mP1.x = mP2.x = offset + (c * (mHistSizeNum + 10) + h) *
      thikness;
    mP1.y = sizeRgba.height-1;
    mP2.y = mP1.y - (int)mBuff[h];
    Core.line(image, mP1, mP2, mColorsRGB[c], thikness);
  }
}
```

The first thing to notice is that we can only compute the histogram for one channel at a time. That's why we have a for loop running for the three channels. As for the body for the loop, the first step is to call `Imgproc.calcHist()` that does all the heavy lifting after passing it to the following arguments:

- A list of Mat objects. `Imgproc.calcHist()` calculates the histogram for a list of images and, in our case, we are passing a list of Mat objects containing only one image.

- A `MatOfInt` object for the channel index.

- A Mat object to be used as a mask in case we want to calculate the histogram for a specific region of the image. However, in our case, we need to calculate the histogram for the whole image and that's why we send an empty Mat object.

- A Mat object to store the histogram values.

- A `MatOfInt` object to hold the number of bins.

- A `MatOfFloat` object to hold the histogram range.

Now that we have computed the histogram, it is necessary to normalize its values so that we can display them on the device screen. `Core.normalize()` can be used in several different ways:

```
Core.normalize(hist, hist, sizeRgba.height/2, 0, Core.NORM_INF);
```

The one used here is to normalize using the norm of the input array, which is the histogram values in our case, passing the following arguments:

- A Mat object as the source of the values to normalize.

- A Mat object as the destination after normalization.

- A double alpha. In the case of a norm normalization, the alpha will be used as the norm value. For the other case, which is a range normalization, the alpha will be the minimum value of the range.

- A double beta. This parameter is only used in the case of a range normalization as the maximum range value. In our case, we passed 0 as it is not used.

- An integer norm type. This argument specifies which normalization to use. In our case, we passed `Core.NORM_INF`, which tells OpenCV to use the infinity norm for normalization, setting the maximum value of the input array to equal the alpha parameter that in our case is set to half of the image height. You could use a different norm such as an L2 norm or L1 norm and this is equivalent to passing `Core.NORM_L2` or `Core.NORM_L1`, respectively. Alternatively, you can use range normalization by passing `Core.MINMAX`, which will normalize the values of the source to be between the alpha and beta parameters.

After normalization, we retrieve the histogram bin values in a float array:

```
hist.get(0, 0, mBuff);
```

Finally, we plot a line for every bin in the histogram using `Core.line()`:

```
for(int h=0; h<mHistSizeNum; h++) {
  //calculate the starting x position related to channel C plus 10
  //pixels spacing multiplied by the thickness
  mP1.x = mP2.x = offset + (c * (mHistSizeNum + 10) + h) *
    thikness;
  mP1.y = sizeRgba.height-1;
  mP2.y = mP1.y - (int)mBuff[h];
  Core.line(image, mP1, mP2, mColorsRGB[c], thikness);
}
```

To `Core.line()`, we pass the following parameters:

- A Mat object to plot on
- A `Point` object representing the starting point of the line
- A `Point` object representing the ending point of the line
- A `Scalar` object representing the line color
- An integer representing the line thickness

The final output would be the loaded image with a histogram for every color channel:

Enhancing the image contrast

Now that you understand what a histogram is and how to calculate it, it is time to look at one of the most widely used image enhancing techniques: the histogram equalization. The histogram equalization technique is used to enhance the image contrast, that is, the difference between the minimum and maximum intensity values in order to strengthen image details that could be washed out.

Understanding histogram equalization

From an abstract point of view, what the histogram equalization does is it finds a function that takes the image's original histogram and transforms it to a stretched histogram with a uniform distribution of the image intensity values, thus enhancing the image contrast.

In practice, histogram equalization doesn't produce a perfectly equalized output histogram; however, it forms a good approximation of the needed transformation that spreads the intensity values more evenly over the defined equalization range of the image:

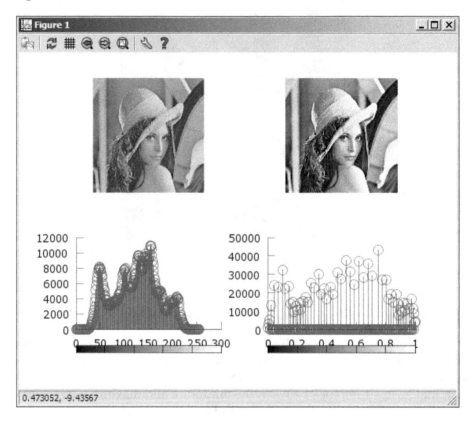

Enhancing grayscale images

Since the beginning of the book, we haven't really distinguished between applying the set of algorithms that we have to a grayscale or full color image. However, applying histogram equalization to a grayscale image has a different effect than applying it to a full color image.

We will start by applying the histogram equalization to the grayscale images first.

UI definitions

We will build on the project that we developed earlier by adding more menu items to trigger the image enhancing functionality.

Open the menu file, `res/menu/iodark_room.xml`, and add the new submenu:

```
<item android:id="@+id/enhance_gs"
  android:title="@string/enhance_gs"
  android:enabled="true"android:visible="true"
  android:showAsAction="always"
  android:titleCondensed="@string/enhance_gs_small">
  <menu>
  <item android:id="@+id/action_togs"
    android:title="@string/action_ctgs"/>
  <item android:id="@+id/action_egs"
    android:title="@string/action_eggsistring"/>
  </menu>
</item>
```

In the new submenu, we added two new items: one to convert the image to grayscale and the second to trigger the histogram equalization.

Converting an image to grayscale

OpenCV supports many color space conversions so the effort needed to convert a full color image to grayscale is very minimal.

We need to update the `onOptionsItemSelected(MenuItem item)` method in the activity to handle pressing the new menu item in order to convert to grayscale:

```
else if (id == R.id.action_togs) {
  if(sampledImage==null)
  {
    Context context = getApplicationContext();
    CharSequence text = "You need to load an image first!";
    int duration = Toast.LENGTH_SHORT;

    Toast toast = Toast.makeText(context, text, duration);
```

```
    toast.show();
    return true;
  }
  greyImage=new Mat();
  Imgproc.cvtColor(sampledImage, greyImage,
    Imgproc.COLOR_RGB2GRAY);
  displayImage(greyImage);
  return true;
}
```

We do a check to see if the sampled image is already loaded and then call `Imgproc.cvtColor()` and pass to it the following parameters:

- A Mat object as our source image.

- A Mat object as the destination image.

- An integer to indicate which color space to convert from and which color space to convert to. In our case, we chose to convert from RGB to grayscale.

Finally, we display the grayscale image.

Equalizing a histogram for a grayscale image

We change the `onOptionsItemSelected(MenuItem item)` method to handle the histogram equalization menu item:

```
else if (id == R.id.action_egs) {
  if(greyImage==null)
  {
    Context context = getApplicationContext();
    CharSequence text = "You need to convert the image to
      greyscale first!";
    int duration = Toast.LENGTH_SHORT;

    Toast toast = Toast.makeText(context, text, duration);
    toast.show();
    return true;
  }
  Mat eqGS=new Mat();
  Imgproc.equalizeHist(greyImage, eqGS);
  displayImage(eqGS);
  return true;
}
```

We will again check to see if the user already converted the image to grayscale; otherwise the histogram equalization method will fail. Then, we call `Imgproc.equalizeHist()` passing in two parameters:

- A Mat object as the source image
- A Mat object as the destination image

Finally, we call `displayImage()` to show the image after the enhancement:

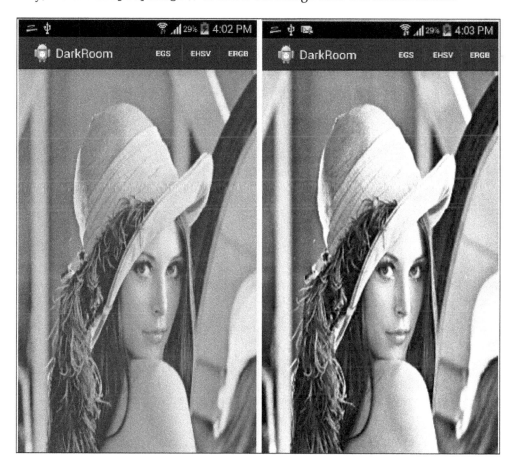

Enhancing an HSV image

To enhance a full color image using histogram equalization and get the same effect, that is, enhancing the image contrast, we need to convert the image from the RGB space to the HSV and then apply the same algorithm to the saturation (S) and value (V) channels.

UI definitions

The changes are related to adding the new menu item to trigger the HSV enhancement:

```
<item android:id="@+id/action_HSV"
  android:titleCondensed="@string/action_enhanceHSV"
  android:title="@string/action_enhanceHSV"android:enabled="true"
  android:showAsAction="ifRoom"android:visible="true"/>
```

Equalizing a histogram for the image saturation and value

The main skill that you need to master is working with image channels on individual bases:

```
else if (id == R.id.action_HSV) {
  if(sampledImage==null)
  {
    Context context = getApplicationContext();
    CharSequence text = "You need to load an image first!";
    int duration = Toast.LENGTH_SHORT;

    Toast toast = Toast.makeText(context, text, duration);
    toast.show();
    return true;
  }
```

First, update onOptionsItemSelected(MenuItem item) to handle the new menu item:

```
Mat V=new Mat(sampledImage.rows(),sampledImage.cols(),
  CvType.CV_8UC1);
Mat S=new Mat(sampledImage.rows(),sampledImage.cols(),
  CvType.CV_8UC1);
```

Initialize two new Mat objects to hold the image value and saturation channels:

```
Mat HSV=new Mat();
Imgproc.cvtColor(sampledImage, HSV, Imgproc.COLOR_RGB2HSV);
```

Now, we convert the RGB image to the HSV color space:

```
byte [] Vs=new byte[3];
byte [] vsout=new byte[1];
byte [] ssout=new byte[1];

for(int i=0;i<HSV.rows();i++){
  for(int j=0;j<HSV.cols();j++)
  {
    HSV.get(i, j,Vs);
    V.put(i,j,new byte[]{Vs[2]});
    S.put(i,j,new byte[]{Vs[1]});
  }
}
```

Then, we access the image pixel by pixel to copy the saturation and value channels:

```
Imgproc.equalizeHist(V, V);
Imgproc.equalizeHist(S, S);
```

Call Imgproc.equalizeHist() to enhance the value and saturation channels:

```
for(int i=0;i<HSV.rows();i++){
  for(int j=0;j<HSV.cols();j++)
  {
    V.get(i, j,vsout);
    S.get(i, j,ssout);
    HSV.get(i, j,Vs);
    Vs[2]=vsout[0];
    Vs[1]=ssout[0];
    HSV.put(i, j,Vs);
  }
}
```

Now, we copy the enhanced saturation and value back to the original image:

```
Mat enhancedImage=new Mat();
Imgproc.cvtColor(HSV,enhancedImage,Imgproc.COLOR_HSV2RGB);
displayImage(enhancedImage);
return true;
```

Finally, we convert the HSV color space to RGB and display the enhanced image:

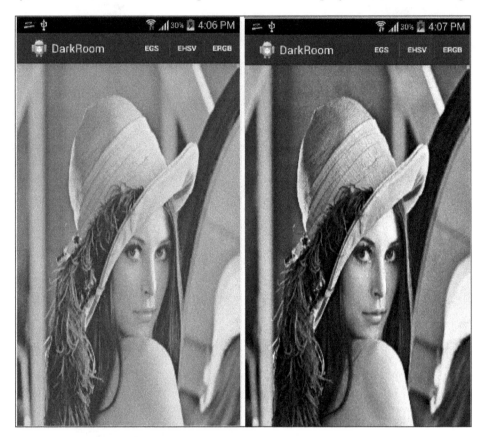

Enhancing an RGB image

Executing histogram equalization on the Red, Green, and Blue channels will give you a different effect as if you are adjusting the color hue.

UI definitions

We will add a new menu item to execute the RGB enhancement on individual channels or a group of channels:

```
<item android:id="@+id/action_RGB"
  android:title="@string/action_RGB"
  android:titleCondensed="@string/action_enhanceRGB_small"
  android:enabled="true"android:showAsAction="ifRoom"
  android:visible="true">
  <menu>
```

```
<item android:id="@+id/action_ER"
  android:titleCondensed="@string/action_enhance_red_small"
  android:title="@string/action_enhance_red"
  android:showAsAction="ifRoom"android:visible="true"
  android:enabled="true"android:orderInCategory="1"/>
<item android:id="@+id/action_EG" android:showAsAction="ifRoom"
  android:visible="true"android:enabled="true"
  android:titleCondensed="@string/action_enhance_green_small"
  android:title-"@string/action_enhance_green"
  android:orderInCategory="2"/>
<item android:id="@+id/action_ERG" android:showAsAction="ifRoom"
  android:visible="true"android:enabled="true"
  android:titleCondensed="@string/
  action_enhance_red_green_small"
  android:title="@string/action_enhance_red_green"
  android:orderInCategory="3"/>
</menu>
</item>
```

Equalizing a histogram for the image color channels

You probably noticed that accessing the image pixel by pixel is slow, especially if the image resolution is high. In this section, we will explore a different technique to work with image channels that is faster as follows:

```
else if(id==R.id.action_ER)
{
  if(sampledImage==null)
  {
    Context context = getApplicationContext();
    CharSequence text = "You need to load an image first!";
    int duration = Toast.LENGTH_SHORT;

    Toast toast = Toast.makeText(context, text, duration);
    toast.show();
    return true;
  }
  Mat redEnhanced=new Mat();
  sampledImage.copyTo(redEnhanced);
  Mat redMask=new Mat(sampledImage.rows(),sampledImage.cols(),
    sampledImage.type(),new Scalar(1,0,0,0));
```

The important line here is initializing redMask, which is a Mat object, with all the channels set to 0 except the first channel, which is the red channel in an RGB image.

Then, we call the `enhanceChannel()` method passing in a copy of the loaded image and channel mask that we created:

```
enhanceChannel(redEnhanced,redMask);
```

In the `enhanceChannel()` method, we first copy the loaded image to another Mat object:

```
private void enhanceChannel(Mat imageToEnhance,Mat mask)
{
  Mat channel=new  Mat(sampledImage.rows(),sampledImage.cols(),CvType.
CV_8UC1);
  sampledImage.copyTo(channel,mask);

  Imgproc.cvtColor(channel, channel, Imgproc.COLOR_RGB2GRAY,1);
  Imgproc.equalizeHist(channel, channel);
  Imgproc.cvtColor(channel, channel, Imgproc.COLOR_GRAY2RGB,3);
  channel.copyTo(imageToEnhance,mask);
}
```

However, this time we pass a mask to the copy method to extract only the designated channel of the image.

Then, we convert the copied channel to a grayscale color space so that the depth is 8-bit and `equalizeHist()` doesn't fail.

Finally, we convert it to an RGB Mat object, replicating the enhanced channel to the Red, Green, and Blue, and then we copy the enhanced channel to the passed argument using the same mask.

You can easily play around with masks that you construct in order to enhance different channels or a combination of channels.

Summary

By now you should have learned about how images are represented and stored in OpenCV. You also developed your own darkroom application, loaded images from your gallery, calculated and displayed their histograms, and executed histogram equalization on different color spaces in order to enhance how the image looks.

In the next chapter, we will develop a new application to utilize more of the OpenCV image processing and computer vision algorithms. We will use algorithms to smooth images and detect ages, lines, and circles.

3
App 2 - Software Scanner

In this chapter, we will start implementing our next application, a software scanner. It allows people to take a photo of, let's say, a receipt, and applies some transformations in order to make it look as if it was scanned.

This application will be divided in two chapters. In this chapter, we will introduce two important topics that will help us to reach our final goal.

The first topic will be about spatial filtering and its definition and applications. You will learn how to reduce image noise, also known as image smoothing. Additionally, you will understand the process of detecting edges (object boundaries) in an image using different algorithms implemented in OpenCV with a high level of abstraction.

The second topic will be about another famous shape analysis technique called the Hough transform. You will learn about the basic idea behind this technique that has made it very popular and widely used, and we will use the OpenCV implementation to start fitting lines and circles to a set of edge pixels.

Spatial filtering

In *Chapter 2*, *App 1 - Building Your Own Darkroom*, we talked about how you can enhance a given image using techniques such as histogram equalization to make the image more pleasing by enhancing the image contrast in different color spaces. In this section, we will discuss another enhancement technique that is usually used as a preprocessing step for many computer vision algorithms, which is spatial filtering.

Before we start with the concept, let's first create a new Android application. We will follow the same steps as in previous chapter; however, we will list the different steps related to naming the application and so on:

1. Create a new Android project and name it `SoftScanner`.
2. Choose a package name; in our example, we used `com.app2.softscanner`.

3. When creating the blank activity, just name it `SoftScanner`.

4. Continue with the steps to link the OpenCV library with the new application.

5. For the UI definitions and permissions, please follow the exact same steps that we used in the previous chapter.

6. For loading the OpenCV library asynchronously and reading an image from your device, please follow the exact same steps in the *Reading an image using OpenCV* section in *Chapter 2, App 1 - Building Your Own Darkroom*.

 Before moving on, make sure that you are able to load the OpenCV library and read and display an image stored on your phone.

Understanding convolution and linear filtering

The main goal of enhancing an image is to make it more appealing and visually acceptable, and the usual things that you need to do are emphasize the edges, reduce the noise, and sometimes introduce a blurry effect.

These kinds of enhancement operations and many others can be achieved through spatial filtering. We use the term spatial here to emphasize that the filtering process takes place on the actual image pixels and differentiate between it and the other filters such as the frequency domain filters. As we move forward, we are not going to talk about the frequency domain filter, so from now on, we will refer to the spatial filters as just filters.

The process that you usually follow to apply a filter to an image is pretty much standard regardless of which filter you are going to use. Simply, for linear filters, we consider each pixel of the original image, usually referring to it as the target pixel, and replace its value with a weighted sum of a specified neighborhood around it. It is called a linear filter because the target pixel's new value is the outcome of a linear combination (weighted sum) of the pixels in its neighborhood.

The weights in the weighted sum are determined by a filter kernel (a mask); this is just a subimage of the size of the neighborhood that we want to consider. The way to calculate the new target pixel's value is by positioning the kernel such that the location of the center weight coincides with the target pixel; then we combine the weighted neighborhood pixels, including the target pixel and its corresponding weight, to get the new value of the target pixel. Finally, we keep on repeating this process for every pixel in the target image.

The mechanics of applying linear filters in the discrete form are also referred to as convolution, and the filter kernels are sometimes described as convolution kernels.

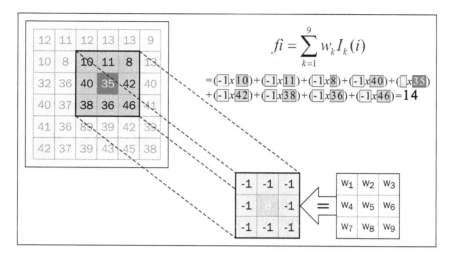

$$fi = \sum_{k=1}^{9} w_k I_k(i)$$

$$= (-1 \times 10) + (-1 \times 11) + (-1 \times 8) + (-1 \times 40) + (\square \times 35)$$
$$+ (-1 \times 42) + (-1 \times 38) + (-1 \times 36) + (-1 \times 46) = 14$$

Finally, we can summarize the linear convolution process as follows:

1. Define the convolution kernel (that is, specify the weights of the neighborhood pixels).

2. Place the kernel on the target image so that the target pixel coincides with the center weight of the kernel.

3. Multiply the pixels beneath the kernel with the corresponding weights in the kernel and replace the target pixel with the outcome.

4. Repeat steps 2 and 3 for every pixel in the target image.

Removing noise

The first application of filtering is blurring an image, also known as smoothing. The outcome of this process is the target image with less noise. We will cover three different blurring techniques: averaging, Gaussian, and median.

The averaging filter

You get the averaging filter by designing the convolution kernel to replace the target pixel's value with the average of the neighborhood under the kernel.

A typical convolution kernel k of size 3×3 would look as this: $k = \dfrac{1}{9} \times \begin{bmatrix} 1 & 1 & 1 \\ 1 & 1 & 1 \\ 1 & 1 & 1 \end{bmatrix}$.

Following the process mentioned before, every target pixel will be replaced by the average of its 3×3 neighborhood and changing the size of the kernel will make the image more blurry as you including more and more pixels in the neighborhood.

The Gaussian filter

The averaging filter treats every pixel in the neighborhood equally so that every pixel in the neighborhood will have the same weight, that is, the same effect on the new target pixel's value.

However, in real situations, this is not the case. Usually, the effect of the neighborhood grows weaker as we move away from the target pixel's location; thus the further you move from the target pixel, the lesser your effect should be, that is, the smaller the weight.

This relationship is achieved using a Gaussian filter. This filter, as the name suggests, uses a Gaussian function to determine the weight distribution of a given neighborhood using the formula for one dimension:

$$f\left(x\right) = ae^{-\frac{(x-b)^2}{2c^2}}$$

This produces a bell curve, where a is the height of the curve's peak, b is the position of the center of the peak or the mean, and c is the standard deviation or sigma, which indicates how wide the bell curve is. An example for a bell curve with parameters is as follows: $[a = 1, b = 0, c = 1]$

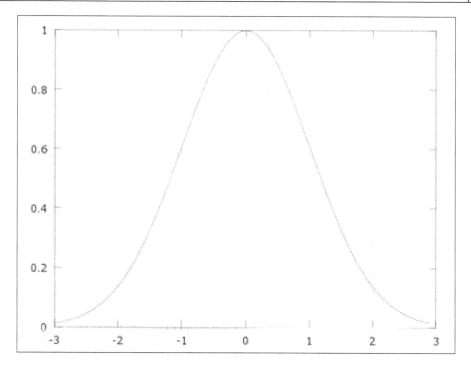

To use the Gaussian function to filter, we should extend it for a two-dimensional space, but without any loss of generality, the same concept applies on the one-dimensional version plotted here.

Now, consider the x axis as the weight index in the kernel (where 0 is the center weight) and the y axis as the weight value. So, if we moved the kernel such that its center (the center of the curve at $x=0$) coincides with the target pixel, then the highest weight (the peak of the curve) will be assigned to the target pixel, and moving away from the center of the kernel, the weights keep on decreasing, thus assigning less importance to the pixel lying further away from the target pixel.

The median filter

In this filter, the pixels in the neighborhood are sorted based on their intensity values, and the target pixel is replaced by the median of the sorted neighborhood. The median filter is very effective in removing a type of noise called the **salt-and-pepper** noise, as shown here:

UI definitions

We will be adding different menu items to our application for every filter type. Go to the `res/menu/soft_scanner.xml` file and open it to include the following menu item:

```
<item
  android:id="@+id/img_blurr"
  android:enabled="true"
  android:orderInCategory="4"
  android:showAsAction="ifRoom"
  android:title="@string/list_blurr"
  android:titleCondensed="@string/list_blurr_small"
```

```
        android:visible="true">
      <menu>
        <item
          android:id="@+id/action_average"
          android:title="@string/action_average"/>
        <item
          android:id="@+id/action_gaussian"
          android:title="@string/action_gaussian"/>
        <item
          android:id="@+id/action_median"
          android:title="@string/action_median"/>
      </menu>
    </item>
```

Applying filters to reduce image noise

OpenCV provides an out-of-the-box implementation for every filter that we discussed here; all we need to do is specify some filter-specific parameters and we are ready to go.

In the `SoftScanner` activity, we need to edit the `onOptionesItemSelected()` method and add the following cases:

```
    else if(id==R.id.action_average)
    {
      if(sampledImage==null)
      {
        Context context = getApplicationContext();
        CharSequence text = "You need to load an image first!";
        int duration = Toast.LENGTH_SHORT;

        Toast toast = Toast.makeText(context, text, duration);
        toast.show();
        return true;
      }
      Mat blurredImage=new Mat();
      Size size=new Size(7,7);
      Imgproc.blur(sampledImage, blurredImage, size);

      displayImage(blurredImage);
      return true;
    }
    else if(id==R.id.action_gaussian)
    {
```

```
    /* code to handle the user not loading an image**/

    /**/
    Mat blurredImage=new Mat();
    Size size=new Size(7,7);
    Imgproc.GaussianBlur(sampledImage, blurredImage, size, 0,0);

    displayImage(blurredImage);
    return true;
}
else if(id==R.id.action_median)
{
    /* code to handle the user not loading an image**/

    /**/
    Mat blurredImage=new Mat();
    int kernelDim=7;
    Imgproc.medianBlur(sampledImage,blurredImage , kernelDim);

    displayImage(blurredImage);
    return true;
}
```

For every selected filter, we follow the same process:

1. We handle the case if the user didn't select or load an image from the gallery:

```
if(sampledImage==null)
{
    Context context = getApplicationContext();
    CharSequence text = "You need to load an image first!";
    int duration = Toast.LENGTH_SHORT;

    Toast toast = Toast.makeText(context, text, duration);
    toast.show();
    return true;
}
```

2. For the averaging filter, we call the `Imgproc.blur()` method passing in the following parameters:
    ° A Mat object for the input image; it could have any number of channels, which are processed independently.

○ A Mat object for the output image after applying the filter.

○ A Size object indicating the size of the kernel (neighborhood) to be used. In our case the kernel will be of size 7×7.

```
Mat blurredImage=new Mat();
Size size=new Size(7,7);
Imgproc.blur(sampledImage, blurredImage, size);
displayImage(blurredImage);
return true;
```

3. To apply a Gaussian filter, we call the `Imgproc.GaussianBlur()` method with the following parameters:

   ○ A Mat object for the input image.

   ○ A Mat object for the output image.

   ○ A Size object indicating the kernel size. You can use a kernel with different height and width; however, both should be odd and positive numbers.

   ○ A double representing the standard deviation in the x direction. In our case, we set it to 0 so that OpenCV computes this value for us depending on the kernel width.

   ○ A double representing the standard deviation in the y direction, also we set it to 0 so that OpenCV calculates the value depending on the kernel height:

```
Mat blurredImage=new Mat();
Size size=new Size(7,7);
Imgproc.GaussianBlur(sampledImage, blurredImage, size,
    0,0);
displayImage(blurredImage);
return true;
```

4. Finally, to use the median filter, we call `Imgproc.medianBlur()` with the following parameters:

   ○ A Mat object for the input image.

   ○ A Mat object for the output image.

- ○ An integer representing the kernel size, and we are using one value because the median filter is a box filter (that is, the kernel width equals its height). However, the value of the kernel dimension should be a positive and odd number.

```
Mat blurredImage=new Mat();
int kernelDim=7;
Imgproc.medianBlur(sampledImage,blurredImage , kernelDim);
displayImage(blurredImage);
return true;
```

The following image shows three examples of applying the averaging filter with different kernel sizes (left: 11, center: 25, and right: 35). You can see that the details start to wash out with increasing kernel size:

The following image is an example of how effective the median filter is in removing the salt-and-pepper noise:

Finding edges

Another application of spatial filtering is finding edges (object boundaries) in images. The process of edge detection is dependent on calculating the rate of a change in pixel intensities. Intuitively, when the rate of change is high, it is more likely that there exists an edge in this area.

To calculate the rate of change, we use the concept of derivative in the discrete domain because for an image of size $n \times n$, we only have row number $1, 2, \ldots, n$ and column number $1, 2, \ldots, n$, and we don't have row number $1.1, 1.2, \ldots, and\ so\ on$.

Let's consider an image $I(x,y)$, where x is the column number and y is the row number. As it is a function of two variables, we will calculate the partial derivative for every variable independently using the following discrete derivative approximation formula for x:

$$\frac{\partial I}{\partial x} = I(x+1,y) - I(x-1,y)$$

This is the first derivative of an image with respect to x, and to calculate the first derivative for the image with respect to y, we use the following equation:

$$\frac{\partial I}{\partial y} = I(x,y+1) - I(x,y-1)$$

So, it is very simple to take the derivative of an image with respect to x. We take the value of a pixel at *x+1* and we subtract it from the pixel at *x-1*, and this is called the central difference and the same applies for y.

Finally, because images have two dimensions (rows and columns), we end up with a gradient vector, $\begin{bmatrix} \frac{\partial I}{\partial x} \\ \frac{\partial I}{\partial y} \end{bmatrix}$, for every pixel (one for the x direction and one for the y direction), and because it is a vector, it can tell us two things:

- The gradient magnitude representing the strength of the edge at this pixel
- The gradient direction representing the edge direction

Moving forward, we can design a simple kernel to calculate the average central difference to find the derivative of an image in the x and y direction as follows:

$$K_x = \frac{1}{3} \times \begin{bmatrix} -1 & 0 & 1 \\ -1 & 0 & 1 \\ -1 & 0 & 1 \end{bmatrix}, K_y = \frac{1}{3} \times \begin{bmatrix} 1 & 1 & 1 \\ 0 & 0 & 0 \\ -1 & -1 & -1 \end{bmatrix}$$

Now, we can summarize the first derivative edge detection process in the following steps:

1. We smooth an image using a smoothing filter (to get rid of the noise).
2. Compute the derivative in the x direction; the output will be an image filtered with a kernel as K_x.

3. Compute the derivative in the y direction; the output will be another image filtered with a kernel as K_y.

4. Calculate the gradient magnitude for every pixel.

5. Threshold the gradient magnitude, that is, if the gradient magnitude of a pixel is greater than a certain threshold, then it is an edge; otherwise, it is not.

The following image is an example to compute the first derivative in the x direction to detect the vertical edges (center) and for the y direction to detect the horizontal edges (right) for the original image (left):

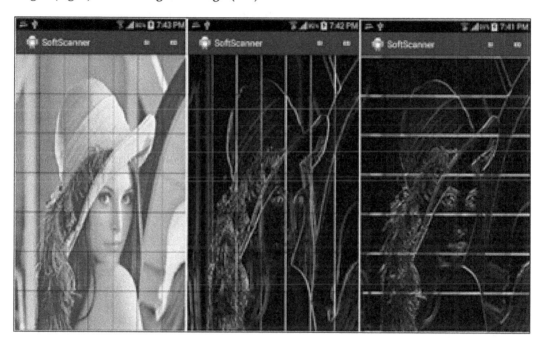

The Sobel edge detector

OpenCV provides you with different edge detectors. The one that we will start with is named **Sobel edge detector**. The main idea here is the design of the convolution kernel:

$$K_x = \begin{bmatrix} -1 & 0 & 1 \\ -2 & 0 & 2 \\ -1 & 0 & 1 \end{bmatrix} \qquad K_y = \begin{bmatrix} -1 & -2 & -1 \\ 0 & 0 & 0 \\ 1 & 2 & 1 \end{bmatrix}$$

The kernel puts more emphasis on the central row for K_x and central column for K_y.

The Canny edge detector

Another very good edge detector also known as the optimal detector is the **Canny edge detector**.

In the Canny edge detector, we decide on an edge pixel in the following steps:

1. We smooth an image using a Gaussian filter.

2. Calculate the gradient vector for every pixel using, for example, a Sobel filter.

3. Suppress the non-maximum pixels by comparing every pixel's gradient magnitude to its neighborhood in the direction of the gradient. We decide that it is a part of an edge, and hence we keep it if its gradient magnitude is the maximum.

4. Finally, Canny uses two thresholds (low and high) for a procedure called hysteresis to decide on the kept pixels:

    ◦   If the gradient magnitude of the pixel is greater than the high threshold, then the pixel is accepted as an edge pixel.

    ◦   The pixel is immediately rejected if its gradient magnitude is less than the low threshold.

    ◦   If the pixel gradient magnitude is between the high and low thresholds and it is connected to a pixel with a gradient magnitude higher than the high threshold, then the pixel will be accepted as an edge pixel.

UI definitions

We will add a few menu items to our application in order to trigger the different edge detectors that we will use. Go to the `res/menu/soft_scanner.xml` file and open it to include the following menu item:

```
<item
   android:id="@+id/img_edge_detection"
   android:enabled="true"
   android:orderInCategory="5"
   android:showAsAction="ifRoom"
   android:title="@string/list_ed"
   android:titleCondensed="@string/list_ed_small"
   android:visible="true">
   <menu>
     <item
       android:id="@+id/action_sobel"
       android:title="@string/action_sobel"/>
```

```
      <item
        android:id="@+id/action_canny"
        android:title="@string/action_canny"/>
    </menu>
</item>
```

Applying the Sobel filter to find edges

In this section, we will use both the Sobel and Canny edge detectors to find edges in images. We will start with the Sobel edge filter.

In the SoftScanner activity, we need to edit the onOptionesItemSelected() method and add the following case:

```
else if(id==R.id.action_sobel)
{
  if(sampledImage==null)
  {
    Context context = getApplicationContext();
    CharSequence text = "You need to load an image first!";
    int duration = Toast.LENGTH_SHORT;

    Toast toast = Toast.makeText(context, text, duration);
    toast.show();
    return true;
  }
  Mat blurredImage=new Mat();
  Size size=new Size(7,7);
  Imgproc.GaussianBlur(sampledImage, blurredImage, size, 0,0);

  Mat gray = new Mat();
  Imgproc.cvtColor(blurredImage, gray, Imgproc.COLOR_RGB2GRAY);

  Mat xFirstDervative =new Mat(),yFirstDervative =new Mat();
  int ddepth=CvType.CV_16S;

  Imgproc.Sobel(gray, xFirstDervative,ddepth , 1,0);
  Imgproc.Sobel(gray, yFirstDervative,ddepth , 0,1);

  Mat absXD=new Mat(),absYD=new Mat();

  Core.convertScaleAbs(xFirstDervative, absXD);
  Core.convertScaleAbs(yFirstDervative, absYD);

  Mat edgeImage=new Mat();
```

```
Core.addWeighted(absXD, 0.5, absYD, 0.5, 0, edgeImage);

displayImage(edgeImage);
return true;
}
```

As Sobel is a first derivative edge detector, we will follow the process outlined earlier:

1. We smooth the image using one of the blurring filters that you learned about earlier to reduce noise responses when we calculate edge pixels. In our case, and for most of the cases, we used a Gaussian filter of size 7×7:

    ```
    Mat blurredImage=new Mat();
    Size size=new Size(7,7);
    Imgproc.GaussianBlur(sampledImage, blurredImage, size, 0,0);
    ```

2. Convert the smoothed image to a grayscale image:

    ```
    Mat gray = new Mat();
    Imgproc.cvtColor(blurredImage, gray, Imgproc.COLOR_RGB2GRAY);
    ```

3. Calculate the x and y first derivatives for the grayscale image using `Imgproc.Sobel()` and passing in the following parameters:

    ○   A Mat object as the source image.

    ○   A Mat object as the output image.

    ○   An integer depth that is used to indicate the depth of the output image. In most of the cases, both the input and output images have the same depth; however, when we calculate the derivative in some cases, the value is negative (that is, moving from white (255) to black (0), $derivative = -255 - 0 = -255$). So, if we are using a Mat object with an unsigned 8-bit depth (gray image only holds a value from 0 to 255), then the value of the negative derivative will overflow and set to 0, that is, we will miss this edge. To work around this issue, we use a signed 16-bit depth output image to store the negative derivatives.

    ○   An integer for the x order that we want to compute. We set it to 1 to compute the first derivative for x.

    ○   An integer for the y order that we want to compute. We set it to 1 to compute the first derivative for y.

 Note that to calculate the gradient in the x direction, we use *x-order=1* and *y-order=0*. We do the same analogously for the y direction.

The following is the code:

```
Mat xFirstDervative =new Mat(),yFirstDervative =new Mat();
int ddepth=CvType.CV_16S;

Imgproc.Sobel(gray, xFirstDervative,ddepth , 1,0);
Imgproc.Sobel(gray, yFirstDervative,ddepth , 0,1);
```

4. We call `Core.convertScaleAbs()` to perform three operations sequentially on the input Mat object:

   ° Scale the input Mat object values; however, as we didn't pass any scaling factors, the scale step is bypassed.

   ° Take the absolute value for every element in the input Mat object. We need this step because we stored the negative values of the x and y first derivatives, but we actually care about the absolute value of the derivatives and we want to be able to store these values in an unsigned 8-bit Mat object (storing values from 0 to 255).

   ° Convert to an unsigned 8-bit depth Mat object.

   The parameters for `Core.convertScaleAbs()` are the input and output Mat objects:

```
Mat absXD=new Mat(),absYD=new Mat();
Core.convertScaleAbs(xFirstDervative, absXD);
Core.convertScaleAbs(yFirstDervative, absYD);
```

5. We try to approximate the gradient magnitude to display the edge image using `Core.addWeighted()`, which calculates the weighted sum of the two images. We achieve this by passing the following parameters:

   ° A Mat object for the first image. We passed the absolute first derivative in the x direction.

   ° A double for the weight of the first image; in our case, it is `0.5` for both the images.

   ° A Mat object for the second image. We passed the absolute first derivative in the y direction.

   ° A double for the weight of the second image.

   ° A double value added to each sum. We don't need to add anything so we send `0`.

   ° A Mat object to store the output image.

This is an approximation for the gradient magnitude. It is good for the purpose of this example; however, if you need to calculate the actual gradient magnitude, you will have to use this formula $gradient\ magnitude = \sqrt{f_x^2 + f_y^2}$, where $f_x\ and\ f_y$ are the values of the first derivative in the x and y directions, respectively.

The following is the code:

```
Mat edgeImage=new Mat();
Core.addWeighted(absXD, 0.5, absYD, 0.5, 0, edgeImage);
```

6. Finally, we display edgeImage:

```
displayImage(edgeImage);
```

An example of applying the Sobel filter to detect edges

Using the Canny edge detector

Applying the Canny edge detector is simpler; we will actually need to execute only one function in OpenCV, and all the steps of the Canny edge detector will be executed for us. With this level of abstraction, we only need to specify some of the algorithm parameters.

In the SoftScanner activity, we need to edit the onOptionesItemSelected() method and add the following case:

```
else if(id==R.id.action_canny)
{
  if(sampledImage==null)
  {
    Context context = getApplicationContext();
    CharSequence text = "You need to load an image first!";
    int duration = Toast.LENGTH_SHORT;

    Toast toast = Toast.makeText(context, text, duration);
    toast.show();
    return true;
  }
  Mat gray = new Mat();
  Imgproc.cvtColor(sampledImage, gray, Imgproc.COLOR_RGB2GRAY);

  Mat edgeImage=new Mat();
  Imgproc.Canny(gray, edgeImage, 100, 200);

  displayImage(edgeImage);
  return true;
}
```

You can see that the steps are much simpler:

1. We convert the input image to grayscale because Canny only works on grayscale images:
```
Mat gray = new Mat();
Imgproc.cvtColor(sampledImage, gray,
  Imgproc.COLOR_RGB2GRAY);
```

2. We call Imgproc.Canny() and pass the following parameters:
    - A Mat object as the input grayscale image
    - A Mat object for the output edge image
    - A double for the lower threshold in the hysteresis step
    - A double for the upper threshold in the hysteresis step

Canny recommends a ratio for the upper and lower thresholds between 2:1 and 3:1.

The following is the code:

```
Mat edgeImage=new Mat();
Imgproc.Canny(gray, edgeImage, 100, 200);
```

3. Finally, we display edgeImage:

```
displayImage(edgeImage);
```

An example of applying the Canny edge detector

Detecting shapes

So, we have seen how to detect edges; however, this process is a pixel-by-pixel process answering the question of whether this pixel is an edge or not. Moving forward, in shape analysis, we would need more concrete information than just the edge test; we will need a better representation.

For example, if we have a picture of a box and we did the edge detection, we will end up with thousands and thousands of edge pixels; however, if we tried to fit a line to these edge pixels, we get a rectangle, which is a more symbolic and useful representation.

Understanding the Hough line transform

There are many ways to fit a line through a number of points, and **Hough transform** is considered an under constrained method, where we use only one point to find all the possible lines that can go through this point and we use another point to find all the lines that can go through it too, and we keep doing this for all the points that we have.

We end up with a voting system where each point is voting for a line and the more points lying on the same line, the higher the votes given to that line. In a nutshell, the Hough transform can be described as mapping a point in the x, y space to the parameter space of the shape of interest.

With the equation of a line in the x and y space, $y = ax + b$, we transform it to the space of the slope (a) and intercept space (b), and given this transformation, a point in the x and y space is actually a line in the slope and intercept space with the equation, $b = (-x)a + y$:

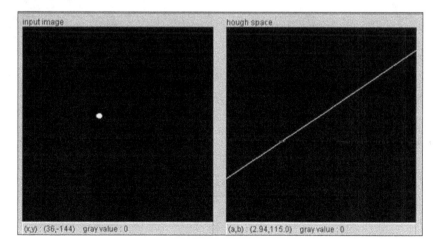

In the following image, we have five points in the x and y space (left). When converted to the slope and intercept space, we get five lines (right):

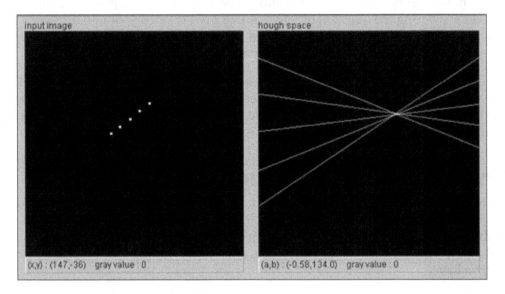

Now, every point in the x and y space will vote for a slope and intercept in the slope and intercept space, so all we have to do is find the maxima in the parameter space and this will be the line to fit our points on:

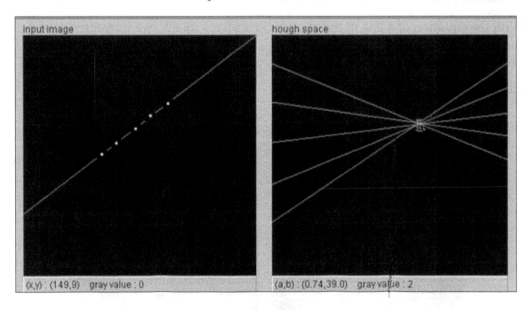

In the right image of preceding image, you can find the maxima value based on the votes of the points in the left image, and in the left image, you can see that the maxima is the slope and intercept of the line fitting the points.

In the case of vertical lines, the slope is infinity and that's why it is more practical to use the polar equation of a line instead the slope and intercept form. In this case, the equation that we will work with is $r = x\cos\theta + y\sin\theta$, and again we have two parameters $r\left(rho\right)$ and θ, and we will follow the same idea except that the space is now r and θ instead of the slope and intercept.

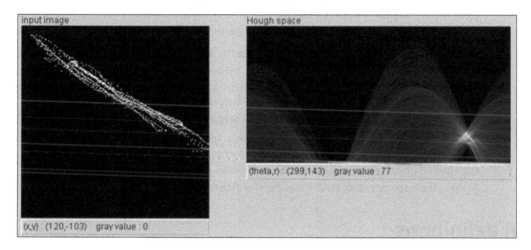

We again follow the voting system to find the maxima that represents r and θ of the line fitting our points. However, this time, a point in the x and y space will be sinusoid, and if two or more sinusoids intersect at the same r and θ, this means that they belong to the same line:

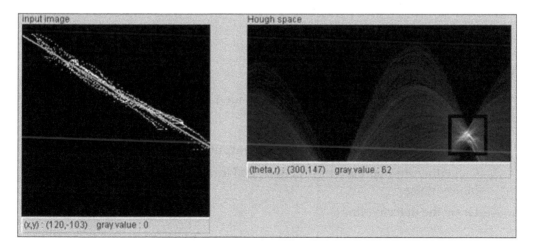

You can see the Hough transform in action using the applets at
`http://www.rob.cs.tu-bs.de/teaching/interactive/`.

Detecting lines using Hough transform

In OpenCV, we have two implementations of the Hough line transform:

1. **The Standard Hough Transform**: The process is pretty much similar to the previously explained process; however, it is considered the slower option as the algorithm has to examine all the edge points in a given image.

2. **The Probabilistic Hough Line Transform**: This option is the one we will use in our example. In the probabilistic version, the algorithm attempts to minimize the amount of computation needed to detect the lines by exploiting the difference in the fraction of votes needed to detect the lines. Intuitively, for strong or long lines, we only need a small fraction of its supporting points to vote before deciding if the accumulator bin reaches a count that is non-accidental. However, for shorter lines, a much higher portion is needed to decide. In conclusion, the algorithm tries to minimize the number of edge points that are needed to decide on the fitting line.

UI definitions

We will add a new menu item to start the Hough transform algorithm. Go to the `res/menu/soft_scanner.xml` file and open it to include the following menu item:

```
<item android:id="@+id/action_HTL"
  android:enabled="true"
  android:visible="true"
  android:title="@string/action_HL">
</item>
```

Detecting and drawing lines

The process to use Hough line transform is divided in four steps:

1. Load the image of interest.
2. Detect image edges using Canny; the output will be a binary image.
3. Call either the standard or probabilistic Hough line transform on the binary image.
4. Draw the detected lines.

In the `SoftScanner` activity, we need to edit the `onOptionesItemSelected()` method and add the following case:

```
else if(id==R.id.action_HTL)
{
  if(sampledImage==null)
  {
    Context context = getApplicationContext();
    CharSequence text = "You need to load an image first!";
    int duration = Toast.LENGTH_SHORT;

    Toast toast = Toast.makeText(context, text, duration);
    toast.show();
    return true;
  }
  Mat binaryImage=new Mat();
  Imgproc.cvtColor(sampledImage, binaryImage,
    Imgproc.COLOR_RGB2GRAY);

  Imgproc.Canny(binaryImage, binaryImage, 80, 100);

  Mat lines = new Mat();
  int threshold = 50;

  Imgproc.HoughLinesP(binaryImage, lines, 1, Math.PI/180,
    threshold);

  Imgproc.cvtColor(binaryImage, binaryImage,
    Imgproc.COLOR_GRAY2RGB);
  for (int i = 0; i < lines.cols(); i++)
  {
    double[] line = lines.get(0, i);
    double xStart = line[0],
    yStart = line[1],
    xEnd = line[2],
    yEnd = line[3];
    org.opencv.core.Point lineStart = new
      org.opencv.core.Point(xStart, yStart);
    org.opencv.core.Point lineEnd = new
      org.opencv.core.Point(xEnd, yEnd);

    Core.line(binaryImage, lineStart, lineEnd, new
      Scalar(0,0,255), 3);
  }
  displayImage(binaryImage);

  return true;
}
```

The code is actually quite straightforward and the following steps are to detect and draw lines:

1. We first handle the case wherein if the user clicks the menu item and doesn't load an image:

```
if(sampledImage==null)
{
   Context context = getApplicationContext();
   CharSequence text = "You need to load an image first!";
   int duration = Toast.LENGTH_SHORT;

   Toast toast = Toast.makeText(context, text, duration);
   toast.show();
   return true;
}
```

2. Then, we initialize a new Mat object and convert the loaded image from the full color space to the grayscale space. Finally, we call `Imgproc.Canny()` to convert the grayscale image to a binary image with only the edges displayed:

```
Mat binaryImage=new Mat();
Imgproc.cvtColor(sampledImage, binaryImage, Imgproc.COLOR_
RGB2GRAY);
Imgproc.Canny(binaryImage, binaryImage, 80, 100);
```

3. The next step is to call `Imgproc.HoughLinesP()`, which is the probabilistic version of the original Hough transform method, passing in the following parameters:

   - A Mat object representing the binary image version of the loaded image
   - A Mat object to hold the detected lines as the parameters $\left(x_{start}, y_{start}, x_{end}, y_{end} \right)$
   - A double for the resolution, in pixels, of the parameter rho; in our case, we set it to be one pixel
   - A double for the resolution, in radians, of the parameter θ; in our case, we set to it to be one degree $\left(\dfrac{\pi}{180} \right)$
   - An integer for the accumulator threshold to return only the lines with enough votes

Usually, when using the probabilistic version of the Hough transform, you would use a smaller threshold because the algorithm is used to minimize the number of points used to vote. However, in the standard Hough transform, you should use a larger threshold.

The following is the code:

```
Mat lines = new Mat();
int threshold = 50;
Imgproc.HoughLinesP(binaryImage, lines, 1, Math.PI/180,
    threshold);
```

4. Finally, we convert the binary image to a full color space in order to display the detected lines, then we loop on the detected lines and draw them one by one using the parameters, $\left(x_{start}, y_{start}, x_{end}, y_{end} \right)$:

```
Imgproc.cvtColor(binaryImage, binaryImage, Imgproc.COLOR_
GRAY2RGB);
for (int i = 0; i < lines.cols(); i++)
{
  double[] line = lines.get(0, i);
  double xStart = line[0],
  yStart = line[1],
  xEnd = line[2],
  yEnd = line[3];
  org.opencv.core.Point lineStart = new
    org.opencv.core.Point(xStart, yStart);
  org.opencv.core.Point lineEnd = new
    org.opencv.core.Point(xEnd, yEnd);

  Core.line(binaryImage, lineStart, lineEnd, new
    Scalar(0,0,255), 3);
}
displayImage(binaryImage);
```

You can note the detected Hough lines in the grid in the following input image:

Hough lines (in blue) detected from the edge image

Detecting circles using Hough transform

OpenCV provides you with another implementation of the Hough transform, but this time, instead of detecting the lines, we detect circles following the same idea of transforming the x, y space to the parameter space.

With the equation of a circle, $r^2 = (x-a)^2 + (y-b)^2$, we have three parameters, $r, a, and\ b$, where a and b are the centers of the circle in the x and y directions, respectively, and r is the radius.

Now, the parameter space is three-dimensional and every edge point belonging to a circle will vote in this three-dimensional space, then we search for the maxima in the parameter space to detect the circle center and radius.

This procedure is very memory- and computation-intensive, and the three-dimensional space will be very sparse. The good news is that OpenCV implements the circle Hough transform using a method called **Hough gradient method**.

The Hough gradient method works as follows: for step one, we apply an edge detector, for example, the Canny edge detector. In step two, we increment the accumulator cells (two-dimensional space) in the direction of the gradient for every edge pixel. Intuitively, if we are encountering a circle, the accumulator cell with the higher votes is actually that circle's center. Now that we have built a list of potential centers, we need to find the circle's radius. So, for every center, we consider the edge pixels by sorting them according to their distance from the center and keep a single radius that is supported (voted for) by the highest number of edge pixels:

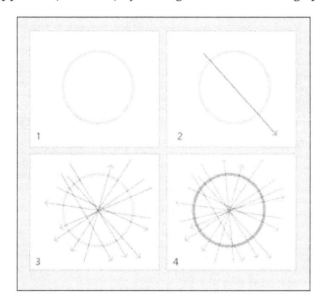

UI definitions

To trigger the circle Hough transform, we will add one menu item to our existing menu. Go to the `res/menu/soft_scanner.xml` file and open it to include the following menu item:

```
<item android:id="@+id/action_CHT"
  android:enabled="true"
  android:visible="true"
  android:title="@string/action_CHT">
</item>
```

Detecting and drawing circles

The process of detecting circles is much similar to the process of detecting lines:

1. Load the image of interest.

2. Convert it from a full color space to a grayscale space.

3. Call the circle Hough transform method on the grayscale image.

4. Draw the detected circles.

We edit `onOptionsItemSelected()` to handle the circle Hough transform case:

```
else if(id==R.id.action_CHT)
{
  if(sampledImage==null)
  {
    Context context = getApplicationContext();
    CharSequence text = "You need to load an image first!";
    int duration = Toast.LENGTH_SHORT;

    Toast toast = Toast.makeText(context, text, duration);
    toast.show();
    return true;
  }
  Mat grayImage=new Mat();
  Imgproc.cvtColor(sampledImage, grayImage,
    Imgproc.COLOR_RGB2GRAY);

  double minDist=20;
  int thickness=5;
  double cannyHighThreshold=150;
  double accumlatorThreshold=50;
  Mat circles = new Mat();
  Imgproc.HoughCircles(grayImage, circles,
    Imgproc.CV_HOUGH_GRADIENT, 1,
    minDist,cannyHighThreshold,accumlatorThreshold,0,0);

  Imgproc.cvtColor(grayImage, grayImage, Imgproc.COLOR_GRAY2RGB);
  for (int i = 0; i < circles.cols(); i++)
  {
    double[] circle = circles.get(0, i);
    double centerX = circle[0],
      centerY = circle[1],
      radius = circle[2];
    org.opencv.core.Point center = new
      org.opencv.core.Point(centerX, centerY);
```

```
    Core.circle(grayImage, center, (int) radius, new
        Scalar(0,0,255),thickness);
    }
    displayImage(grayImage);
    return true;
}
```

The code for the circle Hough transform is just as the one for the detection of lines, except for the following part:

```
double minDist=20;
int thickness=5;
double cannyHighThreshold=150;
double accumlatorThreshold=50;

Mat circles = new Mat();
Imgproc.HoughCircles(grayImage, circles,
    Imgproc.CV_HOUGH_GRADIENT, 1,
    minDist,cannyHighThreshold,accumlatorThreshold,0,0);

Imgproc.cvtColor(grayImage, grayImage, Imgproc.COLOR_GRAY2RGB);
for (int i = 0; i < circles.cols(); i++)
{
    double[] circle = circles.get(0, i);
    double centerX = circle[0],
        centerY = circle[1],
        radius = circle[2];
    org.opencv.core.Point center = new
        org.opencv.core.Point(centerX, centerY);
    Core.circle(grayImage, center, (int) radius, new
        Scalar(0,0,255),thickness);
}
```

We detect circles by calling `Imgproc.HoughCircles()` and passing to it the following parameters:

- A Mat object representing the 8-bit, single-channel grayscale input image.

- A Mat object that will hold the detected circles. Every column of the matrix will hold a circle represented by these parameters, $(x, y, radius)$.

- An integer for the detection method. Currently, OpenCV only implements the Hough gradient algorithm.

- A double used to set the ratio between the accumulator and input image size. For example, if we passed 1, the accumulator will have the same size (width and height) as the input image. If we passed 3, the accumulator size will be one-third of the input image.

- A double for the minimum distance between the centers of the detected circles. Note that the greater the distance, the more true circles you will miss; the shorter the distance, the more false circles you will detect.

- A double used for the upper threshold of the internal Canny edge detector; as for the lower threshold, it will be half the upper one.

- A double for the accumulator threshold for the number of votes for every detected center.

- An integer for the minimum radius that we are looking for; if you don't know it, you can pass 0 instead.

- An integer for the maximum radius to be detected; if unknown, pass 0.

Finally, we loop on the detected circles and draw them one by one using `Core.circle()`.

Summary

In this chapter, we covered the concept of spatial filtering and showed different applications for the convolution kernel from noise reduction to edge detection. We've seen how to use OpenCV to smooth images using the averaging, Gaussian, and median filters. We also used the OpenCV implementation for Sobel and Canny edge detectors. In addition to image smoothing and edge detection, we also covered a well-known shape analysis technique called the Hough transform to fit lines and circles to edge pixels.

In the next chapter, we will continue to develop this application in order to use the concepts to detect edges and fit lines to find the appropriate transformation and do some perspective correction so that the documents that we capture using the device's camera will look as if they were scanned.

4
App 2 - Applying Perspective Correction

In this chapter, we will continue building on the application that we started in *Chapter 3*, *App 2 - Software Scanner*.

We will use the concepts that we've discussed, namely, the edge detection and Hough line transform to do perspective correction to a quadrilateral object. Applying perspective transformation to an object will change the way we see it; this idea will come in handy when you take pictures of documents, receipts, and so on and you want to have a better view of the captured image or a scan-like copy.

We will see how to implement this idea using three different flavors:

- Rigid perspective correction
- Flexible perspective correction
- Manual perspective correction

Image transformations and perspective correction

Images can go through a set of transformations. The simplest ones are listed here.

Translation

Basically, in image coordinates translation, what we do is shift every pixel, p=[x,y], with an amount, t=[t_x, t_y]. For example, we can write the translation for pixel p as $p' = p + t$.

Rotation and translation

In this transformation, we apply rotation to every pixel followed by a translation. This transformation is also known as two-dimensional Euclidean transformation as Euclidean distances are preserved.

We can write this transformation as $p' = Rp + t$, where R is a 2-by-2 matrix, which equals $R = \begin{bmatrix} \cos\theta & -\sin\theta \\ \sin\theta & \cos\theta \end{bmatrix}$ and θ is the angle used for rotation.

Scaled rotation

This is also known as similarity transformation, and in this transformation, we add a scaling factor s so that the transformation can be expressed as $p' = sRp + t$. This transformation preserves the angles between the lines.

Affine

In the Affine transformation, parallel lines remain parallel and it can be expressed as $p' = Ap\tilde{}$, where $p\tilde{} = [x, y, 1]$, and $A = \begin{bmatrix} a & b & c \\ d & e & f \end{bmatrix}$.

Perspective transformation

This is also known as projective transformation, and in this transformation, we use a 3-by-3 matrix instead of a 2-by-3 matrix to change the viewpoint of the pixels. The main difference between Affine and perspective transformation is that the latter doesn't preserve parallel lines, it only preserves their straightness.

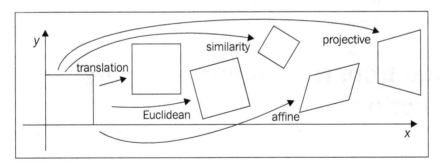

One can argue that the main idea behind perspective correction is finding a perspective transformation matrix that we can apply to an image to get a better view of the object of interest.

To find this matrix, we first need to detect the object of interest using the ideas that we discussed in *Chapter 3, App 2 - Software Scanner*, select a set of interest points, and then specify where these interest points should be in order to have a better view of the object.

An example of this set of points could be the object corners, and we would have the scan-like view if we found a perspective transformation matrix to change these corners' coordinates to correspond to the corners of the device screen.

In the light of the preceding example, we will discuss the three flavors of perspective correction and demonstrate different ways of finding these corners to build the correspondence that we need in order to find the appropriate perspective transformation matrix.

Rigid perspective correction

Our first trial to do perspective correction will be a rigid one. We will follow these steps:

1. Convert the input image to grayscale.

2. Use the Canny edge detector to get the edge image.

3. Detect the lines in the edge image using the probabilistic Hough transform.

4. Find the bounding lines of the object of interest.

5. Estimate the bounding rectangle of the object of interest; hence the name rigid because the object doesn't need to have parallel opposite sides, but we will enforce this by using a rectangular estimation to the quadrilateral object.

6. Build a list of the rectangle's four corners.

7. Impose a correspondence between the rectangle corners and screen corners.

8. Use the correspondence to get a perspective transformation matrix.

9. Apply the transformation matrix to the input image to get the corrected perspective of the object of interest.

UI definitions

We will add an additional menu item to start the perspective correction process. Go to the `res/menu/soft_scanner.xml` file and open it to include the following menu item:

```
<item
  android:id="@+id/action_rigidscan"
  android:enabled="true"
```

```
    android:orderInCategory="6"
    android:title="@string/action_rigidscan"
    android:visible="true">
</item>
```

Estimating the perspective transformation using the object bounding box

In the SoftScanner activity, we need to edit the onOptionesItemSelected() method and add a new case to handle the user by selecting the rigid scan option.

1. The first step is to make sure that the user has already loaded an image:

```
else if(id==R.id.action_rigidscan)
{
  if(sampledImage==null)
  {
    Context context = getApplicationContext();
    CharSequence text = "You need to load an image first!";
    int duration = Toast.LENGTH_SHORT;

    Toast toast = Toast.makeText(context, text, duration);
    toast.show();
    return true;

  }
```

2. Convert the input image to a grayscale image:

```
Mat gray = new Mat();
Imgproc.cvtColor(sampledImage, gray,
  Imgproc.COLOR_RGB2GRAY);
```

3. Use the Canny edge detector to build the edge image:

```
Mat edgeImage=new Mat();
Imgproc.Canny(gray, edgeImage, 100, 200);
```

4. After building the edge image, we need to detect lines, so we use the probabilistic Hough line transform:

```
Mat lines = new Mat();
int threshold = 50;
Imgproc.HoughLinesP(edgeImage, lines, 1,
  Math.PI/180, threshold,60,10);
```

5. Declare and initialize the variables needed to find up to four bounding lines of the object of interest and to discard any lines detected on the object itself in order to have a better estimation of the bounding rectangle:

```
boolean [] include=new boolean[lines.cols()];
double maxTop=edgeImage.rows();
double maxBottom=0;
double maxRight=0;
double maxLeft=edgeImage.cols();
int leftLine=0;
int rightLine=0;
int topLine=0;
int bottomLine=0;
ArrayList<org.opencv.core.Point> points=new ArrayList<org.opencv.
core.Point>();
```

6. In the following `for` loop, we test every line to find the left-most border line of the object of interest. Once it is found, we set its corresponding include array element to true to avoid selecting the same line again when we search for a different bounding line:

```
for (int i = 0; i < lines.cols(); i++)
{
  double[] line = lines.get(0, i);
  double xStart = line[0], xEnd = line[2];
  if(xStart<maxLeft && !include[i])
  {
    maxLeft=xStart;
    leftLine=i;

  }
  if(xEnd<maxLeft && !include[i])
  {
    maxLeft=xEnd;
    leftLine=i;

  }
}
include[leftLine]=true;
```

7. Once the line is found, we add its two points to the `points` array list. This array list will be used later when we estimate the bounding rectangle:

```
double[] line = lines.get(0, leftLine);
double xStartleftLine = line[0],
    yStartleftLine = line[1],
```

```
        xEndleftLine = line[2],
        yEndleftLine = line[3];

    org.opencv.core.Point lineStartleftLine = new org.opencv.core.
    Point(xStartleftLine, yStartleftLine);
    org.opencv.core.Point lineEndleftLine = new org.opencv.core.
    Point(xEndleftLine, yEndleftLine);

    points.add(lineStartleftLine);
    points.add(lineEndleftLine);
```

8. We do the same to find the right-most bounding line:

```
    for (int i = 0; i < lines.cols(); i++)
    {
      line = lines.get(0, i);
      double xStart = line[0], xEnd = line[2];

      if(xStart>maxRight && !include[i])
      {
        maxRight=xStart;
        rightLine=i;

      }
      if(xEnd>maxRight && !include[i])
      {
        maxRight=xEnd;
        rightLine=i;

      }
    }
    include[rightLine]=true;
```

9. Add the points that belong to the right-most border line to the `points` array list:

```
    line = lines.get(0, rightLine);
    double xStartRightLine = line[0],
        yStartRightLine = line[1],
        xEndRightLine = line[2],
        yEndRightLine = line[3];

    org.opencv.core.Point lineStartRightLine = new org.opencv.core.
    Point(xStartRightLine, yStartRightLine);
```

```
org.opencv.core.Point lineEndRightLine = new org.opencv.core.
Point(xEndRightLine, yEndRightLine);

points.add(lineStartRightLine);
points.add(lineEndRightLine);
```

10. Find the top border line:

```
for (int i = 0; i < lines.cols(); i++)
{
  line = lines.get(0, i);
  double yStart = line[1],yEnd = line[3];

  if(yStart<maxTop && !include[i])
  {
    maxTop=yStart;
    topLine=i;
  }
  if(yEnd<maxTop && !include[i])
  {
    maxTop=yEnd;
    topLine=i;

  }
}
include[topLine]=true;
```

11. Add the points that belong to the top border line to the `points` array list:

```
line = lines.get(0, topLine);
double xStartTopLine = line[0],
    yStartTopLine = line[1],
    xEndTopLine = line[2],
    yEndTopLine = line[3];

org.opencv.core.Point lineStartTopLine = new
  org.opencv.core.Point(xStartTopLine, yStartTopLine);

org.opencv.core.Point lineEndTopLine = new
  org.opencv.core.Point(xEndTopLine, yEndTopLine);

points.add(lineStartTopLine);
points.add(lineEndTopLine);
```

12. Find the bottom border line:

```
for (int i = 0; i < lines.cols(); i++)
{
  line = lines.get(0, i);
  double yStart = line[1],yEnd = line[3];
  if(yStart>maxBottom && !include[i])
  {
    maxBottom=yStart;
    bottomLine=i;

  }
  if(yEnd>maxBottom && !include[i])
  {
    maxBottom=yEnd;
    bottomLine=i;
  }
}
include[bottomLine]=true;
```

13. Add the bottom line points to the `points` array list:

```
line = lines.get(0, bottomLine);
double xStartBottomLine = line[0],
    yStartBottomLine = line[1],
    xEndBottomLine = line[2],
    yEndBottomLine = line[3];

org.opencv.core.Point lineStartBottomLine = new
  org.opencv.core.Point(xStartBottomLine,
  yStartBottomLine);

org.opencv.core.Point lineEndBottomLine = new
  org.opencv.core.Point(xEndBottomLine, yEndBottomLine);

points.add(lineStartBottomLine);
points.add(lineEndBottomLine);
```

14. We initialize a matrix of points, `MatOfPoint2f` object, with the list of points that we selected from the detected border lines:

```
MatOfPoint2f mat=new MatOfPoint2f();
mat.fromList(points);
```

15. We find the bounding rectangle by calling `Imgproc.minAreaRect()` and passing in the matrix of points that we initialized earlier. The function tries to find a rectangle that fits a set of points and has the minimum area of all the possible rectangles. As we used the points on the border lines of the object of interest, we will get the bounding rectangle of that object:

```
RotatedRect rect= Imgproc.minAreaRect(mat);
```

16. Now, we extract the four corner points of the estimated rectangle to an array of points:

```
org.opencv.core.Point rect_points[]=new
  org.opencv.core.Point [4];
rect.points(rect_points);
```

17. Initialize a new image that will be used to display the object of interest after doing the perspective correction. We will also use this image's four corners to find the transformation that will minimize the distance between these corners and the corresponding object of interest's corners. So, basically, what we are trying to do is to find a transformation (scale, rotation, or translation) that will make the four corners of the object of interest as close as possible to the four corners of the new initialized image.

```
Mat correctedImage=new Mat(sampledImage.rows(),
  sampledImage.cols(),sampledImage.type());
```

18. Now, we initialize two `Mat` objects, one to store the four corners of the object of interest and the other one to store the corresponding corners of the image in which we will display the object of interest after the perspective correction:

```
Mat srcPoints=Converters.vector_Point2f_to_Mat(
  Arrays.asList(rect_points));
Mat destPoints=Converters.vector_Point2f_to_Mat(
  Arrays.asList(new org.opencv.core.Point[]{
  new org.opencv.core.Point(0,
    correctedImage.rows()),
    new org.opencv.core.Point(0, 0),
    new org.opencv.core.Point(correctedImage.cols(),0),
  new org.opencv.core.Point(correctedImage.cols(),
    correctedImage.rows())
}));
```

19. We calculate the needed transformation matrix by calling `Imgproc.getPerspectiveTransform()` and passing it to the source and destination corner points:

```
Mat transformation=Imgproc.getPerspectiveTransform(
  srcPoints, destPoints);
```

20. Finally, we apply the transformation that we calculated using the `Imgproc.warpPerspective()` method and passing the following arguments:

    ○ A Mat object for the source image; in this case, it is the image that contains the object of interest

    ○ A Mat object for the output image

    ○ A Mat object for the transformation that we want to apply

    ○ A Size object to hold the size of the output image

    ```
    Imgproc.warpPerspective(sampledImage, correctedImage,
        transformation, correctedImage.size());
    ```

21. The last step is to display our object of interest after applying the appropriate transformation:

    ```
    displayImage(correctedImage);
    ```

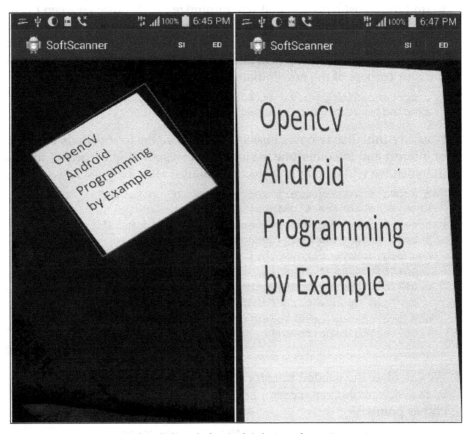

Before (left) and after (right) the transformation

Flexible perspective correction

Now that we have implemented the rigid correction, we want to get slightly better results. As discussed before, the main reason to use the perspective correction is to find the four corner points of the object of interest. In the *Rigid perspective correction* section, we used the estimated bounding rectangle to find the corners of the object of interest; however, as you know, every opposite side of a rectangle is parallel, and this might degrade the results of the perspective correction because parallel lines in the real world have to intersect in what is called a **vanishing point** when projected to the picture plane.

So, having parallel lines to estimate the corners is not our best option and we can do better by keeping the projected lines (the ones that we found from the Hough transform) in the picture as is and use simple geometry to find the intersection between them in order to find the four corners.

The steps that we will perform are as follows:

1. Convert the input image to grayscale and smooth using a Gaussian filter.
2. Find the edge image using the Canny edge detector.
3. Use the probabilistic Hough line transform to find the edge lines of the object of interest.
4. Find every corner in the edge image by computing the intersection points between all the detected lines.
5. Approximate another polygon using the found corners (vertices) in the previous step. This step is necessary to minimize the number of vertices, hence eliminating the non-useful corners. However, we still keep the same structure of the original polygon.
6. Now that we have the minimum set of corners that represent our object of interest, we need to sort them so that the top left corner comes first, then the top right, bottom right, and finally, bottom left.
7. Impose a correspondence between the sorted corners and screen corners.
8. Use the correspondence to get a perspective transformation matrix.
9. Apply the transformation matrix to the input image to get the corrected perspective of the object of interest.

UI definitions

We will use one menu item to start the flexible perspective correction process. Go to the `res/menu/soft_scanner.xml` file and open it to include the following menu item:

```
<item
  android:id="@+id/action_flexscan"
  android:enabled="true"
  android:orderInCategory="7"
  android:title="@string/action_flexscan"
  android:visible="true">
</item>
```

Applying flexible perspective correction

In the `SoftScanner` activity, we need to edit the `onOptionesItemSelected()` method and add a new case for the flexible scan:

1. The first step is to make sure that the user loaded an image:

```
else if(id==R.id.action_flexscan)
{
  if(sampledImage==null)
  {
    Context context = getApplicationContext();
    CharSequence text = "You need to load an image first!";
    int duration = Toast.LENGTH_SHORT;

    Toast toast = Toast.makeText(context, text, duration);
    toast.show();
    return true;
  }
```

2. We follow the same steps as we did in the *Rigid perspective correction* section to get the edge lines:

```
Mat gray = new Mat();
Imgproc.cvtColor(sampledImage, gray,
  Imgproc.COLOR_RGB2GRAY);
Imgproc.GaussianBlur(gray, gray, new Size(7,7), 0);

Mat edgeImage=new Mat();
Imgproc.Canny(gray, edgeImage, 100, 300);

Mat lines = new Mat();
```

```
int threshold = 100;
Imgproc.HoughLinesP(edgeImage, lines, 1,
  Math.PI/180, threshold,60,10);
```

3. We compute the intersection point—if it exists—between every pair of the detected edge lines L_1 defined by two points $(X_1,Y_1),(X_2,Y_2)$ and L_2 defined by two points (X_3,Y_3) and (X_4,Y_4) using the formulas, $IP_x = \left(\dfrac{(x_1y_2 - y_1x_2)(x_2 - x_4) - (x_1 - x_2)(x_2y_4 - y_2x_4)}{(x_1 - x_2)(y_2 - y_4) - (y_1 - y_2)(x_2 - x_4)} \right)$ and

$IP_y = \left(\dfrac{(x_1y_2 - y_1x_2)(y_8 - y_4) - (y_1 - y_2)(x_8y_4 - y_8x_4)}{(x_1 - x_2)(y_8 - y_4) - (y_1 - y_2)(x_8 - x_4)} \right)$:

```
ArrayList<org.opencv.core.Point> corners=new ArrayList<org.opencv.core.Point>();
for (int i = 0; i < lines.cols(); i++)
{
  for (int j = i+1; j < lines.cols(); j++)
  {
    org.opencv.core.Point intersectionPoint =
      getLinesIntersection(lines.get(0, i),
      lines.get(0, j));
    if(intersectionPoint!=null)
    {
      corners.add(intersectionPoint);
    }
  }
}
```

4. Now that we have the intersection points, we need to find another polygon that has the same structure as the detected one, yet with less vertices. To achieve this, we use the `Imgproc.approxPolyDP()` method and we pass the following arguments to it:

    ◦ A Mat object storing the list of corners that we found.

    ◦ A Mat object that will store the new vertices of the approximated polygon.

    ◦ A double representing the maximum distance between the original polygon and approximated one. In this case, we used the `Imgproc.arcLength()` method to calculate the perimeter of the original polygon and multiplied it by a small factor, `0.02`, and used the result to set the maximum distance between the two shapes.

    ○   A Boolean to indicate whether the shape is closed or not, and in our case, it is:

```
MatOfPoint2f cornersMat=new MatOfPoint2f();
cornersMat.fromList(corners);

MatOfPoint2f approxConrers=new MatOfPoint2f();
Imgproc.approxPolyDP(cornersMat, approxConrers,
    Imgproc.arcLength(cornersMat, true)*0.02, true);
```

5. In this step, we just make sure that the approximated polygon has at least four corners:

```
if(approxConrers.rows()<4)
{
  Context context = getApplicationContext();
  CharSequence text = "Couldn't detect an object with four
    corners!";
  int duration = Toast.LENGTH_LONG;

  Toast toast = Toast.makeText(context, text, duration);
  toast.show();
  return true;
}
```

6. We copy the approximated corners in the corners list, then use this list to find the polygon centroid, which we will use to sort the approximated corner points. A good centroid approximation is the average of all the approximated corner points.

```
corners.clear();
Converters.Mat_to_vector_Point2f(approxConrers,corners);
org.opencv.core.Point centroid=new
  org.opencv.core.Point(0,0);
for(org.opencv.core.Point point:corners)
{
  centroid.x+=point.x;
  centroid.y+=point.y;
}
centroid.x/=corners.size();
centroid.y/=corners.size();
```

7. Now, we start sorting the corner points according to the polygon centroid. We first split them into two lists, one will hold the top corners that will have a Y coordinate less than the centroid's, and the second list will hold the bottom corners that will have a Y coordinate greater than the centroid's. Then, we sort the top left and right corners based on the X coordinate in the top corners list, and we do the same for the bottom list:

```
ArrayList<org.opencv.core.Point> top=new
  ArrayList<org.opencv.core.Point>();
ArrayList<org.opencv.core.Point> bottom=new
  ArrayList<org.opencv.core.Point>();

for (int i = 0; i < corners.size(); i++)
{
  if (corners.get(i).y < center.y)
    top.add(corners.get(i));
  else
    bottom.add(corners.get(i));
}

org.opencv.core.Point topLeft = top.get(0).x > top.get(1).x
  ? top.get(1) : top.get(0);

org.opencv.core.Point topRight = top.get(0).x >
  top.get(1).x ? top.get(0) : top.get(1);

org.opencv.core.Point bottomLeft = bottom.get(0).x >
  bottom.get(1).x ? bottom.get(1) :bottom.get(0);

org.opencv.core.Point bottomRight = bottom.get(0).x >
  bottom.get(1).x ? bottom.get(0) : bottom.get(1);

corners.clear();
corners.add(topLeft);
corners.add(topRight);
corners.add(bottomRight);
corners.add(bottomLeft);
```

8. We then build the correspondence between the sorted corners and image corners as we did in the *Rigid perspective correction* section:

```
Mat correctedImage=new Mat(sampledImage.rows(),
  sampledImage.cols(),sampledImage.type());
Mat srcPoints=Converters.vector_Point2f_to_Mat(corners);

Mat destPoints=Converters.vector_Point2f_to_Mat
  (Arrays.asList(new org.opencv.core.Point[]{
  new org.opencv.core.Point(0, 0),
  new org.opencv.core.Point(correctedImage.cols(), 0),
  new org.opencv.core.Point(correctedImage.cols()
    ,correctedImage.rows()),new org.opencv.core.Point
  (0,correctedImage.rows())}));
```

9. We calculate the needed transformation matrix by calling `Imgproc.getPerspectiveTransform()` and passing it in the source and destination corner points:

```
Mat transformation=Imgproc.
  getPerspectiveTransform(srcPoints, destPoints);
```

10. We apply the transformation that we calculated using the `Imgproc.warpPerspective()` method:

```
Imgproc.warpPerspective(sampledImage,
  correctedImage, transformation, correctedImage.size());
```

11. Finally, we display our object of interest after applying the appropriate transformation:

```
displayImage(correctedImage);
```

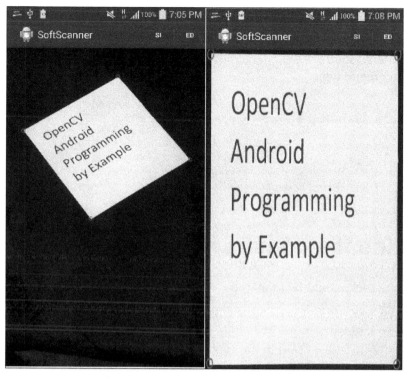

Before (left) and after (right) the transformation

Manual perspective correction

One more option that we can include is making use of the device's touchscreen and making the user select the corners of the object of interest manually. This option could come in handy if there is too much background noise and the automatic perspective correction didn't give the desired results.

The steps that we will follow are very similar to what we have seen in the *Flexible perspective correction* section:

1. Let the user select the four corners of the object of interest.
2. Find the object centroid.
3. Sort the select corners according to the object centroid.
4. Impose a correspondence between the sorted corners and screen corners.
5. Use the correspondence to get a perspective transformation matrix.
6. Apply the transformation matrix to the input image to get the corrected perspective of the object of interest.

UI definitions

We will add one more menu item to trigger the manual process after the user selects the four corners. Go to the res/menu/soft_scanner.xml file and open it to include the following menu item:

```
<item
  android:id="@+id/action_manScan"
  android:enabled="true"
  android:orderInCategory="8"
  android:title="@string/action_manscan"
  android:visible="true">
</item>
```

Selecting the corners manually

We will follow the same process after the user selects the object of interest's corners. However, the trick would be to map the coordinates selected on the device screen to the coordinates of the object of interest:

1. In the activity onCreate() method, we will attach an onTouch() event handler to ImageView. In the event handler, we first project the coordinates of the selected corners from ImageView to the loaded image using the scale factor that we used to display the loaded image. Once we have the correct coordinates on the loaded image, the following steps will be identical to what we did before:

```
final ImageView iv = (ImageView)
findViewById(R.id.SSImageView);
iv.setOnTouchListener(new OnTouchListener() {

  @Override
  public boolean onTouch(View view, MotionEvent event) {

    int projectedX = (int)((double)event.getX() *
      ((double)sampledImage.width()/
      (double)view.getWidth()));

    int projectedY = (int)((double)event.getY() *
      ((double)sampledImage.height()/
      (double)view.getHeight()));

    org.opencv.core.Point corner = new
      org.opencv.core.Point(projectedX, projectedY);
```

```
      corners.add(corner);

      Core.circle(sampledImage, corner, (int) 5, new
        Scalar(0,0,255),2);

      displayImage(sampledImage);
      return false;
    }
  });
```

2. We need to make sure that the user loaded an image and selected the four corners:

```
if(sampledImage==null)
{
  Context context = getApplicationContext();
  CharSequence text = "You need to load an image first!";
  int duration = Toast.LENGTH_SHORT;

  Toast toast = Toast.makeText(context, text, duration);
  toast.show();
  return true;
}
if(corners.size()!=4)
{
  Context context = getApplicationContext();
  CharSequence text = "You need to select four corners!";
  int duration = Toast.LENGTH_LONG;

  Toast toast = Toast.makeText(context, text, duration);
  toast.show();
  return true;
}
```

3. Calculate the object centroid and sort the four corners accordingly:

```
org.opencv.core.Point centroid=new
  org.opencv.core.Point(0,0);
for(org.opencv.core.Point point:corners)
{
  centroid.x+=point.x;
  centroid.y+=point.y;
}
centroid.x/=corners.size();
centroid.y/=corners.size();
sortCorners(corners,centroid);
```

4. We then build the correspondence between the sorted corners and image corners as we did in the *Flexible perspective correction* section:

```
Mat correctedImage=new Mat(sampledImage.rows(),
  sampledImage.cols(),sampledImage.type());
Mat srcPoints=Converters.vector_Point2f_to_Mat(corners);

Mat destPoints=Converters.vector_Point2f_to_Mat
  (Arrays.asList(new org.opencv.core.Point[]{
  new org.opencv.core.Point(0, 0),
  new org.opencv.core.Point(correctedImage.cols(), 0),
  new org.opencv.core.Point(correctedImage.cols()
    ,correctedImage.rows()),
  new org.opencv.core.Point(0,correctedImage.rows())}));
```

5. We calculate the needed transformation matrix by calling `Imgproc.getPerspectiveTransform()` and passing it in the source and destination corner points:

```
Mat transformation=Imgproc.getPerspectiveTransform
  (srcPoints, destPoints);
```

6. We apply the transformation that we calculated using the `Imgproc.warpPerspective()` method:

```
Imgproc.warpPerspective(sampledImage, correctedImage,
  transformation, correctedImage.size());
```

7. Finally, we display our object of interest after applying the appropriate transformation:

```
displayImage(correctedImage);
```

Summary

We've seen how to change the view of an object in an image using the perspective transformation. We demonstrated the idea on quadrilateral objects and we discussed three different ways to do the perspective correction.

In the next chapter, we will explore different types of image features and how we can find them and why they are important.

5
App 3 - Panoramic Viewer

In this chapter, we will start working on a new application. The goal of the application is to stitch two images together in order to form a panoramic view. We will introduce the concept of image features and why they are important, and we will see them in action.

We can summarize the topics that we will cover as follows:

- Feature detection
- Feature description
- Feature matching
- Image stitching

Image features

In this section, we will understand what we mean by image features and why they are important.

Imagine a case where you see a person and you immediately detect the face of the person—his eyes, nose, and many other facial features. The question is how do we do this? What is the algorithm that we follow to detect these facial features? How do we describe them? Additionally, when we see another person with the same facial features, we can easily spot the matching features between the two persons. What is the metric that we use to measure this similarity?

We simply follow the process of detecting, describing, and matching the features. From the computer's perception, we want the process to be able to find features that can be repeatedly extracted, adequately represented, and accurately matched.

These features are considered good features, and to measure the goodness of a feature, we should consider its robustness and invariance (especially, invariance to scale and rotation; for example, our facial features, such as our eyes, are invariant to change in the face scale; whether the face is small or big, you can easily detect where the eyes are). Usually, to achieve such robustness, we consider the quality attributes of the feature detected combined with the quality attributes of the method used to describe it.

For example, we will see some feature detectors, namely **Harris** and **FAST**, find features at mono-scale (single scale), while others such as **ORB** find features at multiscale by building what is known as scale space.

I find this a nice opportunity to introduce the basic idea of the scale space, which is to build an image pyramid using different scale reduction methods. The simplest method would be to remove every other pixel in the X and Y directions. So, for example, if you have a 100x100 image, removing every other pixel from the x and y will result in an image of size 50x50. You keep repeating this step until you reach the minimum acceptable scale that your program will work with.

Feature detectors

The question to begin with is which features are good features in the context of a computer's vision? To answer this question, let's take the image of a mountaintop as an example. We can start looking at features inside the boundaries of this mountain (rectangle 2), but the problem is that these kinds of features can't be repeatedly found nor adequately described, and hence, they will be very difficult to match.

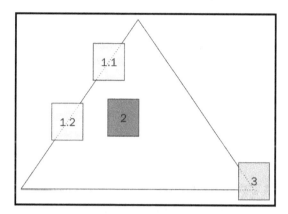

Another candidate to look for is the edges of the mountain; we've learned in *Chapter 3, App 2 - Software Scanner* how to detect edges, so this type of features can be easily found. However, the problem would be how to uniquely describe them, because if you look at rectangles 1.1 and 1.2, you can easily confuse them for the same edge. This problem is known as the aperture problem, and again, it will be very difficult to match.

What about rectangle 3? This rectangle looks like a good option, because if you move it in any direction, the area beneath it will look different and so it is unique. Based on this, we can say that corners are good features to consider.

Understanding the Harris corner detector

We answered the question of which features are good features and we gave an example of a good feature. Now, we need to find a way to easily detect them. So, let's consider the mountaintop image. If we start scanning the image with a square window, the corners will have the maximum change in intensities, because there will be a change in two orthogonal directions unlike the edge, where there will be a change in only one direction (x or y).

This is the basic idea behind the Harris corner detector; we try to find a patch where it will give us the maximum change or variation in intensities if we moved our scanning window in a different direction inside this patch.

The Harris corner detector is rotation invariant; however, it is not scale invariant.

UI definitions

After we create a new application with a blank activity named `PanoActivity` and add the functionality of loading images from the device gallery along with loading the OpenCV library, we will add the first menu item to execute the Harris corner detector on the loaded image. Go to the `res/menu/pano.xml` file and open it to include the following menu item:

```
<itemandroid:id="@+id/action_harris"
  android:orderInCategory="2"
  android:title="@string/action_harris">
</item>
```

Using the Harris corner detector

OpenCV provides you with different interest points or feature detectors, and the API has a very simple interface to work with the class `org.opencv.features2d`. `FeatureDetector` has a factory method, and given a detector ID, the factory method will return an instance of a feature detector corresponding to this ID.

We update `onOptionsItemSelected` to handle the Harris menu item:

```
if(sampledImage==null)
{
  Context context = getApplicationContext();
  CharSequence text = "You need to load an image first!";
  int duration = Toast.LENGTH_SHORT;

  Toast toast = Toast.makeText(context, text, duration);
  toast.show();
  return true;
}

Mat greyImage=new Mat();
MatOfKeyPoint keyPoints=new MatOfKeyPoint();
Imgproc.cvtColor(sampledImage, greyImage, Imgproc.COLOR_RGB2GRAY);

FeatureDetector detector =
  FeatureDetector.create(FeatureDetector.HARRIS);
```

```
detector.detect(greyImage, keyPoints);

Features2d.drawKeypoints(greyImage, keyPoints, greyImage);

displayImage(greyImage);
```

The steps are very simple, as follows:

1. We first convert the input image to grayscale and instantiate a matrix of the key points object:

```
Mat greyImage=new Mat();
MatOfKeyPoint keyPoints=new MatOfKeyPoint();
Imgproc.cvtColor(sampledImage, greyImage,
  Imgproc.COLOR_RGB2GRAY);
```

2. We instantiate the feature detector of our choice using the `FeatureDetector.create` factory method and passing its ID:

```
FeatureDetector detector =
  FeatureDetector.create(FeatureDetector.HARRIS);
```

3. Call the `detect` method using the following command:

```
detector.detect(greyImage, keyPoints);
```

The detect method is called to find the interest points with the following parameters:

   ° A Mat object representing the input image
   ° A `MatOfKeyPoint` object to store the detected interest points

4. To display the detected interest points, we call `Feature2d.drawKeypoints()`:

```
Features2d.drawKeypoints(greyImage, keyPoints, greyImage);
```

We call `Feature2d.drawKeypoints()` with the following parameters:

   ° A Mat object as the input image
   ° A `MatOfKeyPoint` to be drawn
   ° A Mat object for the output image

5. Finally, display the image with the interest points detected:

```
displayImage(greyImage);
```

Calling a native Harris corner detector

In many cases, your application will need to respond in real time, such as detecting features in a video feed from your phone's camera. Relying only on Java calls might not deliver the performance that you desire and hence, missing your deadlines. In this case, it is more than 20 frames per second; and that's why I find this a nice opportunity to introduce you to the native OpenCV API. You don't need to be familiar with C++; however, knowing the language constructs will be very helpful.

The first thing that we will need to do is add C++ support to our project.

Using the native OpenCV library within Eclipse

1. Right-click on the project name in the project explorer.

2. Navigate to **New | Other | C/C++ | Convert to a C/C++ Project**.

3. Select `Makefile project`, choose **Other Toolchain**, and click on **Finish**:

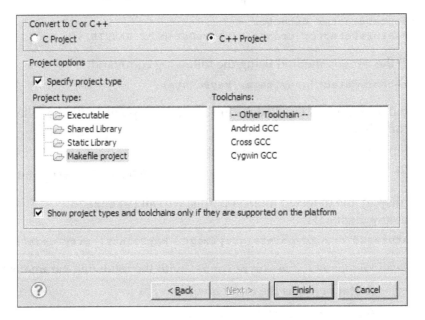

4. Define an environment variable, `NDKROOT`, pointing to the home folder of NDK, for example, `C:\NVPACK\android-ndk-r10c`.

5. Right-click on the project name in the project explorer and select **Properties**.

6. Click on the tree node, **C/C++ Build**. In the **Builder Setting** tab, clear the **Use default build command** checkbox and write the following in the **Build command** textbox: `${NDKROOT}/ndk-build.cmd`.

7. Go to the **Behaviour** tab, and in the **Workbench Build Behavior** group, check **Build on resource save** and clear the **Make build target** textbox. Clear **Make build target** textbox for the **Build (Incremental build)** checkbox:

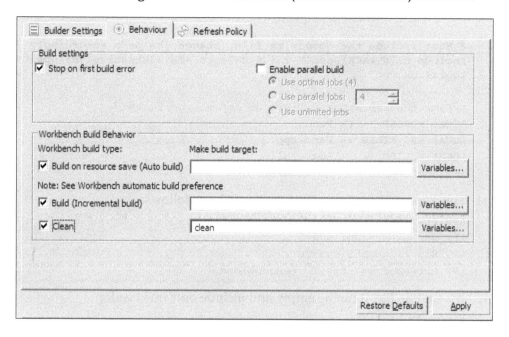

8. At this point, invoking NDK to build your project will fail, and to fix this, we need to create a new folder under the project folder and name it `jni`.

9. In this folder, we will have three files:

10. The content of `Android.mk` should be as follows:

```
LOCAL_PATH := $(call my-dir)

include$(CLEAR_VARS)

# Must include the opencv.mk file, change the path accordingly
include C:\NVPACK\OpenCV-2.4.8.2-Tegra-sdk\sdk\native\jni\OpenCV-
tegra3.mk

# Name the library and list the cpp source files
LOCAL_MODULE    := Pano
LOCAL_SRC_FILES := Pano.cpp
LOCAL_LDLIBS += -llog -ldl
include$(BUILD_SHARED_LIBRARY)
```

11. The content of `Application.mk` should be as follows:

```
APP_PLATFORM := android-9
APP_ABI := armeabi-v7a
APP_STL := gnustl_static
APP_CPPFLAGS := -frtti -fexceptions
```

12. For the cpp file, it can be empty and include only one header:

```
#include <jni.h>
```

13. Build the project.

14. We need to include some directories so that we can write C++ code and use the **Standard Template Library** (**STL**) and OpenCV. To do this, right-click on the project name | **Properties** | **C/C++ General** | **Paths and Symbols**.

 The STL provides you with a set of ready-made classes that implements different data structures and algorithms.

15. Select **GNU C++**, add the following directories, and change the paths according to your installation:

```
${NDKROOT}/platforms/android-9/arch-arm/usr/include
${NDKROOT}/sources/cxx-stl/gnu-libstdc++/4.6/include
${NDKROOT}/sources/cxx-stl/gnu-libstdc++/4.6/libs/
   armeabi-v7a/include
C:\NVPACK\OpenCV-2.4.8.2-Tegra-sdk\sdk\native\jni\include
```

Using the native OpenCV library within Android Studio

1. In the project view, right-click on the app node and select **Open Module Settings,** or press *F4*.

2. Select **SDK location**. In **Android NDK location**, select the directory where NDK is located. Note that we will build the project using the experimental Gradle plugin version 2.5; hence we need NDK version r10e:

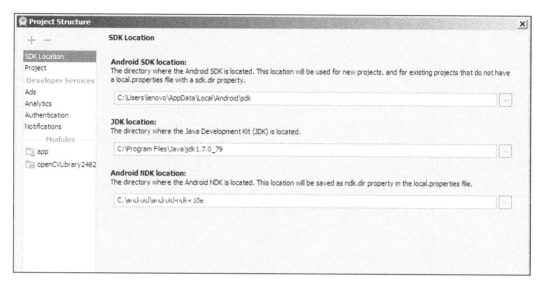

3. If you are working with Android Studio 1.3.2, you will need to update `gradle-wrapper.properties` and change the distribution URL as follows:

   ```
   distributionUrl=https\://services.gradle.org/distributions/gradle-
   2.5-all.zip
   ```

4. In the `build.gradle` file for the project, update the dependency class path as follows:

   ```
   dependencies {classpath
     'com.android.tools.build:gradle-experimental:0.2.0'}
   ```

5. In the project folder, create two folders, `jni` and `jniLibs` under `app\src\main`.

6. In the `jni` folder, create a new file and name it `Pano.cpp`.

7. Now, navigate to `<OpenCV4AndroidSDKFolder>\sdk\native\libs\` and copy all the folders to your newly created `jniLibs` folder. Your project tree should look as follows:

8. We need to update **domain-specific language (DSL)** in `build.gradle` in order for our module to work with Gradle 2.5. To do so, update the build file to match the following and keep the dependencies method as is. Note that you will need to update the absolute paths to match your installations:

```
applyplugin: 'com.android.model.application' model {
  android {
    compileSdkVersion = 23 buildToolsVersion = "23.0.1"
      defaultConfig.with {
    applicationId = "com.app3.pano"
      minSdkVersion.apiLevel = 15
      targetSdkVersion.apiLevel = 19 versionCode = 1
      versionName = "1.0"
    }
  }
  //Make sure to build with JDK version 7
  compileOptions.with {
    sourceCompatibility=JavaVersion.VERSION_1_7
      targetCompatibility=JavaVersion.VERSION_1_7
  }
```

```
android.ndk {
  moduleName = "Pano" ldLibs += ['log']
  cppFlags += "-std=c++11" cppFlags += "-fexceptions"
    cppFlags += "-I${file("<OpenCV4AndroidSDK_Home>/sdk/
    native/jni/include")}".toString()
  cppFlags += "-I${file("<OpenCV4AndroidSDK_Home>/sdk/
    native/jni/include/opencv")}".toString()
  ldLibs += ["android", "EGL", "GLESv2", "dl", "log",
    "z"]// , "ibopencv_core" stl = "gnustl_shared"}
  android.buildTypes {
    release {
      minifyEnabled= false proguardFiles+=
        file('proguard-rules.pro')
    }
  }
  android.productFlavors {
    create("arm") {
      ndk.with {
        abiFilters += "armeabi" File curDir =
          file('./')
        curDir = file(curDir.absolutePath)
        String libsDir = curDir.absolutePath+"\\src\\
          main\\jniLibs\\armeabi\\" //"-L" + ldLibs +=
          libsDir + "libopencv_core.a" ldLibs +=
          libsDir + "libopencv_imgproc.a" ldLibs +=
          libsDir + "libopencv_java.so" ldLibs +=
          libsDir + "libopencv_features2d.a"
      }
    }
    create("armv7") {
      ndk.with {
        abiFilters += "armeabi-v7a" File curDir =
          file('./')
        curDir = file(curDir.absolutePath)
        String libsDir = curDir.absolutePath+"\\src\\
          main\\jniLibs\\armeabi-v7a\\" //"-L" + ldLibs
          += libsDir + "libopencv_core.a" ldLibs +=
          libsDir + "libopencv_imgproc.a" ldLibs +=
          libsDir + "libopencv_java.so" ldLibs +=
          libsDir + "libopencv_features2d.a"
      }
    }
    create("x86") {
      ndk.with {
        abiFilters += "x86"
      }
```

```
        }
        create("mips") {
          ndk.with {
            abiFilters += "mips"
          }
        }
        create("fat") {
        }
      }
    }
  }
```

9. Finally, we need to update the `build.gradle` file for the OpenCV module in order to match the following:

```
apply plugin: 'com.android.model.library' model {
  android {
    compileSdkVersion = 23 buildToolsVersion = "23.0.1"
      defaultConfig.with {
      minSdkVersion.apiLevel = 15
        targetSdkVersion.apiLevel = 19
    }
  }
  //Make sure to build with JDK version 7
  compileOptions.with {
    sourceCompatibility=JavaVersion.VERSION_1_7
      targetCompatibility=JavaVersion.VERSION_1_7
  }
  android.buildTypes {
    release {
      minifyEnabled= false proguardFiles+=
        file('proguard-rules.pro')
    }
  }
}
```

10. Now, sync and build the project.

Working on the native part

Regardless of the IDE of your choice, you can follow these steps to add the native code to the application:

1. Open `Pano.cpp` and add the following code; we will go through the code later:

```cpp
#include<jni.h>
#include<opencv2/core/core.hpp>
#include<opencv2/imgproc/imgproc.hpp>
#include<opencv2/features2d/features2d.hpp>
#include<vector>

extern"C" {

  JNIEXPORT void JNICALL
    Java_com_app3_pano_PanoActivity_FindHarrisCorners(
    JNIEnv*, jobject, jlong addrGray, jlong addrRgba)
  {
    cv::Mat& mGr  = *(cv::Mat*)addrGray;
    cv::Mat& mRgb = *(cv::Mat*)addrRgba;

    cv::Mat dst_norm;
    cv::Mat dst = cv::Mat::zeros(mGr.size(),CV_32FC1);

    //the size of the neighbor in which we will check
    //the existence of a corner
    int blockSize = 2;
    //used for the Sobel kernel to detect edges before
    //checking for corners
    int apertureSize = 3;
    // a free constant used in Harris mathematical formula
    double k = 0.04;
    //corners response threshold
    float threshold=150;

    cv::cornerHarris( mGr, dst, blockSize, apertureSize, k,
      cv::BORDER_DEFAULT );

    cv::normalize( dst, dst_norm, 0, 255, cv::NORM_MINMAX,
      CV_32FC1, cv::Mat() );

    for( unsignedint i = 0; i < dst_norm.rows; i++ )
    {
      float * row=dst_norm.ptr<float>(i);
```

```
        for(int j=0;j<dst_norm.cols;j++)
        {
          if(row[j]>=threshold)
          {
            cv::circle(mRgb, cv::Point(j, i), 10,
              cv::Scalar(255,0,0,255));
          }
        }
      }
    }
}
```

2. We declare a native method in the PanoActivity class so that we can call the native code later:

```
public native void FindHarrisCorners(long matAddrGr, long
matAddrRgba);
```

3. We build the native library and declare the native method in our activity, but when we try to call the native method, we receive java.lang. UnsatisfiedLinkError, because we haven't loaded the native library yet. To do so, we change the onManagerConnected() method to load the native library after the OpenCV initialization:

```
private BaseLoaderCallback mLoaderCallback = new
  BaseLoaderCallback(this) {
  @Override
  public void onManagerConnected(int status) {
    switch (status) {
      case LoaderCallbackInterface.SUCCESS:
      {
        Log.i(TAG, "OpenCV loaded successfully");
        // Load native library after(!) OpenCV
          initialization
        System.loadLibrary("Pano");
      } break;

      default:
      {
        super.onManagerConnected(status);
      } break;
    }
  }
};
```

4. Now, we are ready to use the native library using a menu item to trigger the native Harris corner detector. So, open `res/menu/pano.xml` and add the following menu item:

```
<itemandroid:id="@+id/action_nativeHarris"
  android:orderInCategory="2"
  android:title="@string/action_nativeHarris">
</item>
```

5. In `PanoActivity`, change `onOptionsItemSelected()` to handle the native case:

```
else if(id==R.id.action_nativeHarris)
{
  if(sampledImage==null)
  {
    Context context = getApplicationContext();
    CharSequence text = "You need to load an image first!",
    int duration = Toast.LENGTH_SHORT;

    Toast toast = Toast.makeText(context, text, duration);
    toast.show();
    return true;
  }

  Mat greyImage=new Mat();
  Imgproc.cvtColor(sampledImage, greyImage,
    Imgproc.COLOR_RGB2GRAY);

  FindHarrisCorners(greyImage.getNativeObjAddr(),
    sampledImage.getNativeObjAddr());

  displayImage(sampledImage);
}
```

We've listed the steps needed to invoke the native implementation of the Harris corner detector; however, we still need to go through the details of the C++ code to get a sense of what we did so that you can extend and build on the ideas that you learn here. Of course, having a basic idea of the C++ language constructs will be very beneficial.

1. We first include a list of the header files that we need:

```
#include<opencv2/core/core.hpp>
#include<opencv2/imgproc/imgproc.hpp>
#include<opencv2/features2d/features2d.hpp>
#include<vector>
```

2. Declare the function we will use following this naming convention, `Java_Fully_Qualified_Class_Name_MethodName`. The method that we declared in `PanoActivity` takes only two parameters: the addresses of the grayscale and colored image; however, the native method takes four. The first two are always used in any JNI method declaration. The second two correspond to the addresses that we sent (`jlong` is mapped to `long` in Java):

```
JNIEXPORT void JNICALL
   Java_com_app3_pano_PanoActivity_FindHarrisCorners(
   JNIEnv*, jobject, jlong addrGray, jlong addrRgba)
```

3. We cast the references that we sent to Mat references, one for the grayscale image and one for the colored:

```
cv::Mat& mGr  = *(cv::Mat*)addrGray;
cv::Mat& mRgb = *(cv::Mat*)addrRgba;
```

4. We declare and initialize a list of variables that we will use to detect the corners:

```
cv::Mat dst_norm;
cv::Mat dst = cv::Mat::zeros(mGr.size(),CV_32FC1);
int blockSize = 2;
intapertureSize = 3;
double k = 0.04;
float threshold=150;
```

5. We call the native implementation for the Harris corner detector and normalize the corners' responses to be between 0 and 255:

```
cv::cornerHarris( mGr, dst, blockSize, apertureSize, k,
   cv::BORDER_DEFAULT );
cv::normalize( dst, dst_norm, 0, 255, cv::NORM_MINMAX,
   CV_32FC1, cv::Mat() );
```

6. We loop on the normalized corners and draw a circle for the detected corner in case its response is greater than the threshold:

```
for( unsignedint i = 0; i < dst_norm.rows; i++ )
{
  float * row=dst_norm.ptr<float>(i);
  for(int j=0;j<dst_norm.cols;j++)
  {
    if(row[j]>=threshold)
    {
    cv::circle(mRgb, cv::Point(j, i), 10,
      cv::Scalar(255,0,0,255));
    }
  }
}
```

The left image is HCD using Java wrappers and the right image is native HCD

Understanding the FAST corner detector

When it comes to real-time applications, there are better detectors in terms of speed. In this section, we will describe how the FAST corner detector works.

Let's consider a pixel, P. We say that P is a potential interest point or a corner if we test 16 pixels in a circular neighborhood of pixel P, and 12 of them have intensities either greater than or less than P's intensity plus/minus a threshold.

This process is computationally expensive, so to speed up the detection, another test was proposed. The algorithm first tests only 4 pixels at specific locations (1, 9, 5, 13); if three of them are greater than or less than P's intensity plus/minus the threshold, and then proceeds with the other 8 pixels; otherwise this pixel is discarded:

UI definitions

Add the following menu item to `res/menu/pano.xml`:

```
<itemandroid:id="@+id/action_fast"
  android:orderInCategory="4"
  android:title="@string/action_fast">
</item>
```

Using the FAST corner detector

Open `PanoActivity` and edit `onOptionsItemSelected()` to include the following case:

```
else if(id==R.id.action_fast)
{
  if(sampledImage==null)
  {
    Context context = getApplicationContext();
    CharSequence text = "You need to load an image first!";
    int duration = Toast.LENGTH_SHORT;

    Toast toast = Toast.makeText(context, text, duration);
```

```
    toast.show();
    return true;
}

Mat greyImage=new Mat();
Imgproc.cvtColor(sampledImage, greyImage,
    Imgproc.COLOR_RGB2GRAY);

MatOfKeyPoint keyPoints=new MatOfKeyPoint();
    FeatureDetector detector=FeatureDetector.create(
        FeatureDetector.FAST);

    detector.detect(greyImage, keyPoints);
    Features2d.drawKeypoints(greyImage, keyPoints, greyImage);
    displayImage(greyImage);
}
```

As we described earlier, OpenCV has a very simple interface and factory method to build different detectors. The only difference between the Harris detector and FAST is the following parameter that we send to the factory method:

```
FeatureDetector detector =
    FeatureDetector.create(FeatureDetector.FAST);
```

The rest of the code is exactly the same.

Using native FAST

In this section, we will add another native method to the `PanoActivity` class in order to call the native implementation to the FAST corner detector:

1. Open the activity class and add the following declaration:

    ```
    public native void FindFastFeatures(long matAddrGr, long
    matAddrRgba);
    ```

    This method takes two arguments; the first is the address of the grayscale image and the second is the address for the colored version.

2. Add the following method to the `Pano.cpp` file:

    ```
    JNIEXPORT void JNICALL
        Java_com_app3_pano_PanoActivity_FindFastFeatures(JNIEnv*,
        jobject, jlong addrGray, jlong addrRgba)
    {
        cv::Mat& mGr  = *(cv::Mat*)addrGray;
        cv::Mat& mRgb = *(cv::Mat*)addrRgba;
    ```

```
std::vector<cv::KeyPoint> v;

cv::FastFeatureDetector detector(50);
detector.detect(mGr, v);
for( unsignedint i = 0; i < v.size(); i++ )
{
  const cv::KeyPoint& kp = v[i];
  cv::circle(mRgb, cv::Point(kp.pt.x, kp.pt.y), 10,
    cv::Scalar(255,0,0,255));
}
}
```

In the preceding code, we first instantiate a vector of key points and a FastFeatureDetector object with a threshold of 50 and call the detection method by passing in the grayscale image and the empty vector of key points. Then, we draw a circle for every detected key point.

3. We add one more menu item to res/menu/pano.xml:

```
<itemandroid:id="@+id/action_nativefast"
  android:orderInCategory="5"
  android:title="@string/action_fastnative">
</item>
```

4. Finally, open PanoActivity and edit onOptionsItemSelected() to include the following case:

```
else if(id==R.id.action_nativefast)
{
  if(sampledImage==null)
  {
    Context context = getApplicationContext();
    CharSequence text = "You need to load an image first!";
    int duration = Toast.LENGTH_SHORT;

    Toast toast = Toast.makeText(context, text, duration);
    toast.show();
    return true;
  }

  Mat greyImage=new Mat();
  Imgproc.cvtColor(sampledImage, greyImage,
    Imgproc.COLOR_RGB2GRAY);
  FindFastFeatures(greyImage.getNativeObjAddr(),
    sampledImage.getNativeObjAddr());

  displayImage(sampledImage);
}
```

The left image is FAST using Java wrappers and the right image is native FAST

Understanding the ORB feature detector

Another important detector, and also a descriptor, came from the OpenCV labs as an alternative for two very famous, yet patented, algorithms (**Scale Invariant Feature Transform** (**SIFT**) and **Speeded Up Robust Features** (**SURF**)), the ORB. To use SIFT and SURF, you need to pay; however, ORB provides a free, good alternative in computation cost and matching performance.

In this section, we will discuss the detector part of the ORB. It mainly uses the FAST algorithm that we saw in the previous section with the following few important additions:

- ORB first uses the FAST algorithm to detect interest points or corners
- It uses Harris to assign a score for every corner (based on the variation of intensities around the detected corner)
- It sorts the scored interest points and considers only the top N corners

- It uses the image pyramid to produce multiscale interest points instead of the mono-scale interest points detected by FAST
- It computes an intensity-weighted centroid for the interest points' neighborhood
- With the interest point and centroid, the algorithm computes this vector direction and assigns it as the interest point orientation; this step is important for the description part of the algorithm

UI definitions

Add the following menu item to `res/menu/pano.xml`:

```
<itemandroid:id="@+id/action_orb"
  android:orderInCategory="6"
  android:title="@string/action_orb">
</item>
```

Using the ORB feature detector

We need to edit `onOptionsItemSelected()` in the `PanoActivity` class to include the following case:

```
else if(id==R.id.action_orb)
{
  if(sampledImage==null)
  {
    Context context = getApplicationContext();
    CharSequence text = "You need to load an image first!";
    int duration = Toast.LENGTH_SHORT;

    Toast toast = Toast.makeText(context, text, duration);
    toast.show();
    return true;
  }

  Mat greyImage=new Mat();
  Imgproc.cvtColor(sampledImage, greyImage,
    Imgproc.COLOR_RGB2GRAY);
  MatOfKeyPoint keyPoints=new MatOfKeyPoint();

  FeatureDetector detector =
    FeatureDetector.create(FeatureDetector.ORB);

  detector.detect(greyImage, keyPoints);
  Features2d.drawKeypoints(greyImage, keyPoints, greyImage);
  displayImage(greyImage);
}
```

It is very simple to switch between the different feature detectors. We just pass the ID of the ORB to the factory method and call the detect method.

Using native ORB

In this section, we will use the native implementation of the ORB detector and move the preprocessing steps to the CPP file in order to reduce the JNI calls overhead to only one call:

1. Open the `PanoActivity` class and add the following declaration:

   ```
   public native void FindORBFeatures(long matAddrRgba, int
     featuresNumber);
   ```

   The method takes two arguments, the address of native object and maximum number of features to detect.

2. In `Pano.cpp`, add the following method implementation:

   ```
   JNIEXPORT void JNICALL
     Java_com_app3_pano_PanoActivity_FindORBFeatures(JNIEnv*,
     jobject, jlong addrRgba, jint featuresNumber)
   {
     cv::Mat& mRgb = *(cv::Mat*)addrRgba;
     cv::Mat grayImg;
     std::vector<cv::KeyPoint> v;

     cv::cvtColor(mRgb,grayImg,cv::COLOR_RGBA2GRAY);

     cv::OrbFeatureDetector detector(featuresNumber);

     detector.detect(grayImg, v);

     cv::drawKeypoints(grayImg,v,mRgb,cv::Scalar::all(
       -1),cv::DrawMatchesFlags::DRAW_RICH_KEYPOINTS);
   }
   ```

   We moved the preprocessing step of converting the colored image to grayscale to `Pano.cpp`. We achieved this by calling `cv::cvtColor` and passing the input image, output image, and mapping code. Then, we instantiated an `ORBFeatureDetector` object with a maximum number of features that equals the parameter we sent.

   In the next line, we call the detect method. Finally, we draw the key points using the `cv::drawKeypoints` method and passing the input image (the one used to detect the key points), vector of `KeyPoint`, output image, color used to draw the key points (using `cv::Scalar::all(-1)` means that the used colors will be random), and finally a flag to use as a circle for every key point with a size that equals the key point size and draw the key point orientation.

3. Add the following menu item to `res/menu/pano.xml`:

```
<itemandroid:id="@+id/action_nativeorb"
  android:orderInCategory="7"
  android:title="@string/action_orbnative">
</item>
```

4. Finally, open `PanoActivity` and edit `onOptionsItemSelected()` to include the following case:

```
else if(id==R.id.action_nativeorb)
{
  if(sampledImage==null)
  {
    Context context = getApplicationContext();
    CharSequence text = "You need to load an image first!";
    int duration = Toast.LENGTH_SHORT;

    Toast toast = Toast.makeText(context, text, duration);
    toast.show();
    return true;
  }

  Mat copy=sampledImage.clone();
  FindORBFeatures(copy.getNativeObjAddr(),100);
  displayImage(copy);
}
```

The left image is ORB using Java wrappers and the right image is
native ORB with feature scale and orientation

Feature description and matching

The second step in the process of using image features is feature description. The feature descriptors are used to provide you with more information around the interest points and are computed over the local region/neighborhood of the detected feature.

Feature descriptors can be categorized with respect to the local region shape (rectangle or circle), sampling pattern (dense sampling, where all the pixels in the local region will contribute to the feature description or sparse sampling, where only the selected pixels will be used), and spectra (binary, where the description vector will only be ones and zeros or scalar using any scalar value or other values).

OpenCV provides feature descriptors belonging to different categories; however, in this section, we will focus only on sparse, binary descriptors (also known as local binary descriptors) due to the fact that SIFT and SURF (dense and scalar) descriptors are patent algorithms and you have to pay to use them.

The local binary descriptors are computed regardless of the descriptor shape, using the pixel pair sampling method, where selected pairs of pixels are compared in order to yield a binary string representing the description vector. For example, if we have a pair of pixels (P1, P2), we compare the intensity of P1 and P2. If P1's intensity is greater than P2, then we put 1 in the description vector, otherwise we insert 0.

Understanding BRIEF and ORB feature descriptors

The **Binary Robust Independent Elementary Features** (**BRIEF**) descriptor is considered the simplest and first local binary descriptor that was proposed. To describe an interest point with a description vector of length N, the algorithm chooses N random pairs of pixels in the 31x31 patch region by several randomization methods (uniform, Gaussian, and others) and compares them to construct the binary string.

As for the ORB, the descriptor adds orientation to BRIEF by steering the interest point to the canonical orientation (given that we know the interest point dominant orientation in the detection stage) and then calculates the description; as a result, we achieve some rotation invariance. For example, if the interest point dominant orientation is 90 degrees, the interest point and its neighborhood are rotated to point upwards (orientation=zero) before ORB is used to describe it, and then the interest point is described so that we can achieve rotation invariance.

For the pixels pair sampling method, ORB learned, offline, to choose the pixel pairs in a way that maximizes the variance and reduces the correlation so that every chosen pixel adds new information to the descriptor.

Using the randomization method (BRIEF) or the learned sampling method (ORB) to choose the pixel pairs results in a nonsymmetrical descriptor shape, as follows:

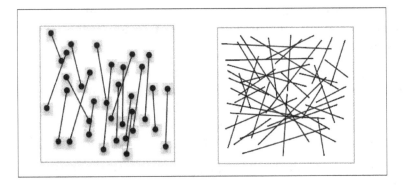

Understanding the BRISK feature descriptor

The **Binary Robust Invariant Scalable Keypoints (BRISK)** descriptor is built on 60 points arranged in four concentric rings, hence the point-pair sampling shape is circular and symmetric. Each point represents a circular sampling area (to choose the sampling pairs) that increases in size as we move away from the interest point.

To calculate the orientation, every sampling region is smoothed with a Gaussian filter and local gradients are calculated. The sampling pairs are divided into two groups: long segments, where the distances between the pairs are above a certain threshold and are used with the local gradients to calculate the orientation angle in order to steer the interest point so that we can achieve rotation invariance. The second category is short segments, where the distances between the pairs are below another threshold and are used to construct a 512-bit binary descriptor by comparing 512 pairs. Following is a figure depicting the distribution of BRISK sampling regions:

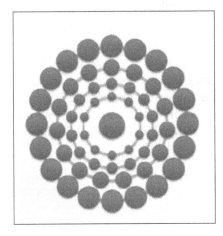

Understanding the FREAK feature descriptor

The **Fast Retina Keypoint** (**FREAK**) descriptor's circular shape is based on the human retinal system, where the density of the receptor cells is the highest at the center and decreases as we move away. As for the sampling pattern, the best pairs of pixels are learned using an offline training algorithm to maximize the point-pairs variance and minimize the correlation.

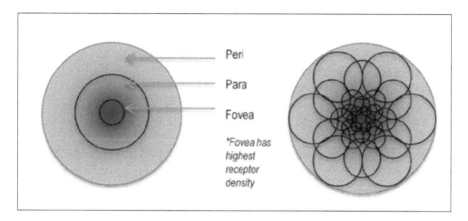

Matching the features

Once you decide on the descriptor that fits your needs, you will need to choose a distance function to determine feature matching. There are many distance functions to use depending on which descriptor you choose. In the case of local binary features, the favorite choice would be the **Hamming distance** to measure the difference between two equal-length binary strings. The operation is very efficient and fast because it can be executed using machine language instructions or an XOR operation followed by a bit count.

Working with feature matching

In this section, we will update the application so that you can mix and match different detectors with different descriptors to find the matching features.

UI definitions

We will define two groups in the application menu. One will be for the set of detectors that we use and the other will be for the set of descriptors. We will also add one more menu item where you can select an object to find in a given scene. Open `res/menu/pano.xml` and add the following items:

```
<item android:orderInCategory="8" android:id="@+id/detector"
    android:title="@string/list_detector">
```

```
        <menu><group android:checkableBehavior="single">
          <item android:id="@+id/harris_check"
            android:title="@string/action_harris"/>
          <item android:id="@+id/fast_check"
            android:title="@string/action_fast" android:checked="true"/>
          <item android:id="@+id/orbD_check"
            android:title="@string/action_orb" />
        </group></menu>
      </item>

      <item android:orderInCategory="9" android:id="@+id/descriptor"
        android:title="@string/list_descriptor">
        <menu><group android:checkableBehavior="single">
          <item android:id="@+id/BRIEF_check"
            android:title="@string/action_brief"/>
          <item android:id="@+id/ORB_check"
            android:title="@string/action_orb" android:checked="true"/>
          <item android:id="@+id/BRESK_check"
            android:title="@string/action_brisk"/>
          <item android:id="@+id/FREAK_check"
            android:title="@string/action_freak"/>
        </group></menu>
      </item>

      <item android:id="@+id/action_match"
        android:orderInCategory="10"
        android:title="@string/action_match">
      </item>

      <item
        android:id="@+id/action_selectImgToMatch"
        android:orderInCategory="1"
        android:showAsAction="never"
        android:title="@string/action_selectImgToMatch"/>
```

Finding an object in a scene

We will follow this process to find an object in a given scene. First, you load the scene, then you load the object image, and finally, select match. To execute the matching process, we edit onOptionsItemSelected() to include the following case:

```
    else if(id==R.id.action_match)
    {
      if(sampledImage==null || imgToMatch==null)
      {
```

```
    Context context = getApplicationContext();
    CharSequence text = "You need to load an object and a scene to
      match!";
    int duration = Toast.LENGTH_SHORT;
    Toast toast = Toast.makeText(context, text, duration);
    toast.show();
    return true;
}

int maximumNuberOfMatches=10;
Mat greyImage=new Mat();
Mat greyImageToMatch=new Mat();

Imgproc.cvtColor(sampledImage, greyImage,
  Imgproc.COLOR_RGB2GRAY);
Imgproc.cvtColor(imgToMatch, greyImageToMatch,
  Imgproc.COLOR_RGB2GRAY);

MatOfKeyPoint keyPoints=new MatOfKeyPoint();
MatOfKeyPoint keyPointsToMatch=new MatOfKeyPoint();

FeatureDetector detector=FeatureDetector.create(detectorID);
detector.detect(greyImage, keyPoints);
detector.detect(greyImageToMatch, keyPointsToMatch);

DescriptorExtractor dExtractor =
  DescriptorExtractor.create(descriptorID);
Mat descriptors=new Mat();
Mat descriptorsToMatch=new Mat();

dExtractor.compute(greyImage, keyPoints, descriptors);
dExtractor.compute(greyImageToMatch, keyPointsToMatch,
  descriptorsToMatch);

DescriptorMatcher matcher = DescriptorMatcher.create(
  DescriptorMatcher.BRUTEFORCE_HAMMING);
MatOfDMatch matches=new MatOfDMatch();
matcher.match(descriptorsToMatch,descriptors,matches);

ArrayList<DMatch> goodMatches=new ArrayList<DMatch>();
List<DMatch> allMatches=matches.toList();

double minDist = 100;
for( int i = 0; i < descriptorsToMatch.rows(); i++ )
{
```

```
        double dist = allMatches.get(i).distance;
        if( dist < minDist ) minDist = dist;
    }

    for( int i = 0; i < descriptorsToMatch.rows() &&
      goodMatches.size()<maximumNuberOfMatches; i++ )
    {
      if(allMatches.get(i).distance<= 2*minDist)
      {
        goodMatches.add(allMatches.get(i));
      }
    }

    MatOfDMatch goodEnough=new MatOfDMatch();
    goodEnough.fromList(goodMatches);
    Mat finalImg=new Mat();
    Features2d.drawMatches(greyImageToMatch, keyPointsToMatch,
      greyImage, keyPoints, goodEnough, finalImg,Scalar.all(-1),
      Scalar.all(-1),new MatOfByte(), Features2d.DRAW_RICH_KEYPOINTS
      + Features2d.NOT_DRAW_SINGLE_POINTS);
    displayImage(finalImg);
}
```

1. We first make sure that the scene and the object images are loaded:

```
if(sampledImage==null || imgToMatch==null)
{
  Context context = getApplicationContext();
  CharSequence text = "You need to load an object and a scene to
match!";
  int duration = Toast.LENGTH_SHORT;
  Toast toast = Toast.makeText(context, text, duration);
  toast.show();
  return true;
}
```

2. Convert both the scene and object image to grayscale:

```
Imgproc.cvtColor(sampledImage, greyImage, Imgproc.COLOR_RGB2GRAY);
Imgproc.cvtColor(imgToMatch, greyImageToMatch, Imgproc.COLOR_
RGB2GRAY);
```

3. Construct a detector object based on the selection made from the application menu and use it to detect features in both the scene and object image:

```
MatOfKeyPoint keyPoints=new MatOfKeyPoint();
```

```
MatOfKeyPoint keyPointsToMatch=new MatOfKeyPoint();

FeatureDetector detector =
   FeatureDetector.create(detectorID);
detector.detect(greyImage, keyPoints);
detector.detect(greyImageToMatch, keyPointsToMatch);
```

4. We do the same thing for the type of descriptor that we use. OpenCV has a descriptor interface similar to the detector one. You call one create method on the `DescriptorExtractor` class and pass the ID of the descriptor that you want to use. In our case, the ID is based on the selection that we make from the application menu.

```
DescriptorExtractor dExtractor =
   DescriptorExtractor.create(descriptorID);
```

5. Next, we compute the description for each feature detected in the scene and the object image by calling the compute method on the descriptor object that we created and passing the image, detected key points, and an empty Mat object to store the description:

```
Mat descriptors=new Mat();
Mat descriptorsToMatch=new Mat();
dExtractor.compute(greyImage, keyPoints, descriptors);
dExtractor.compute(greyImageToMatch, keyPointsToMatch,
   descriptorsToMatch);
```

6. Then, we construct a matcher object by calling the create method on the `DescriptorMacther` class and passing the ID of the distance function of your choice. In our case, we are using local binary descriptors; hence, the Hamming distance will be our favorite choice:

```
DescriptorMatcher matcher = DescriptorMatcher.create(
   DescriptorMatcher.BRUTEFORCE_HAMMING);
```

7. Now, we are ready to find the matching features from the scene and object images by calling the match method on the matcher object and passing the object feature description, scene feature description, and an empty matrix of `DMatch` objects. The `DMatch` object is a simple data structure used to store two matching descriptors and their distance (in our case, the Hamming distance):

```
MatOfDMatch matches=new MatOfDMatch();
matcher.match(descriptorsToMatch,descriptors,matches);
```

8. Finally, we select the best matching points and draw them:

```
ArrayList<DMatch> goodMatches=new ArrayList<DMatch>();
List<DMatch> allMatches=matches.toList();

double minDist = 100;
for( int i = 0; i <descriptorsToMatch.rows(); i++ )
{
  double dist = allMatches.get(i).distance;
  if( dist < minDist ) minDist = dist;
}

for( int i = 0; i <descriptorsToMatch.rows() &&
  goodMatches.size()<maximumNuberOfMatches; i++ )
{
  if( allMatches.get(i).distance<= 2*minDist)
  {
    goodMatches.add(allMatches.get(i));
  }
}

MatOfDMatch goodEnough=new MatOfDMatch();
goodEnough.fromList(goodMatches);

Mat finalImg=new Mat();
Features2d.drawMatches(greyImageToMatch, keyPointsToMatch,
  greyImage, keyPoints, goodEnough,
  finalImg,Scalar.all(-1),Scalar.all(-1),new MatOfByte(),
  Features2d.DRAW_RICH_KEYPOINTS +
  Features2d.NOT_DRAW_SINGLE_POINTS);

displayImage(finalImg);
```

Using ORB for feature detection and description is invariant to scale and rotation

Native feature matching

We've seen how to detect, describe, and match features using the Java wrappers; however, it would be faster if we can group these steps into a single JNI call because the process requires many steps and every step is translated to an individual JNI call to the native code.

In this section, we will execute the feature detection, description, and matching process in the native side of the application.

UI definitions

We will add a new menu item in order to execute the native process. Open `res/menu/pano.xml` and add the following item:

```
<itemandroid:id="@+id/action_native_match"
  android:orderInCategory="11"
  android:title="@string/action_native_match">
</item>
```

The native matching process

In this section, we will move the process and preprocessing steps to the native side of the application; thereby, reducing the overall JNI overhead to a minimum:

1. We first declare a new native method in the activity class. The native method takes a reference to the object image, scene image, detector ID, and descriptor ID and returns an image with the matching results:

```
public native void FindMatches(long objectAddress, long
  sceneAddress,int detectorID, int descriptorID,long
  matchingResult);
```

2. We define the native method in the `Pano.cpp` file:

```
JNIEXPORT void JNICALL
  Java_com_app3_pano_PanoActivity_FindMatches(JNIEnv*,
  jobject, jlong objectAddress, jlong sceneAddress,jint
  detectorID, jint descriptorID,jlong matchingResult)
{
  cv::Mat& object  = *(cv::Mat*)objectAddress;
  cv::Mat& scene = *(cv::Mat*)sceneAddress;
  cv::Mat& result = *(cv::Mat*)matchingResult;
  cv::Mat grayObject;
  cv::Mat grayScene;

  //Convert the object and scene image to grayscale
  cv::cvtColor(object,grayObject,cv::COLOR_RGBA2GRAY);
  cv::cvtColor(scene,grayScene,cv::COLOR_RGBA2GRAY);

  std::vector<cv::KeyPoint> objectKeyPoints;
  std::vector<cv::KeyPoint> sceneKeyPoints;
  cv::Mat objectDescriptor;
  cv::Mat scenceDescriptor;

  //Construct a detector object based on the input ID
  if(detectorID==1)//FAST
  {
```

```
    cv::FastFeatureDetector detector(50);
    detector.detect(grayObject, objectKeyPoints);
    detector.detect(grayScene, sceneKeyPoints);
}
else if(detectorID==5)//ORB
{
    cv::OrbFeatureDetector detector;
    detector.detect(grayObject, objectKeyPoints);
    detector.detect(grayScene, sceneKeyPoints);
}

//Construct a descriptor object based on the input ID
if(descriptorID==3)//ORB
{
    cv::OrbDescriptorExtractor descriptor;
    descriptor.compute(
        grayObject,objectKeyPoints,objectDescriptor);
    descriptor.compute(
        grayScene,sceneKeyPoints,scenceDescriptor);
}
else if(descriptorID==4)//BRIEF
{
    cv::BriefDescriptorExtractor descriptor;
    descriptor.compute(grayObject,objectKeyPoints,
        objectDescriptor);
    descriptor.compute(grayScene,sceneKeyPoints,
        scenceDescriptor);
}
else if(descriptorID==5)//BRISK
{
    cv::BRISK descriptor;
    descriptor.compute(grayObject,objectKeyPoints,
        objectDescriptor);
    descriptor.compute(grayScene,sceneKeyPoints,
        scenceDescriptor);
}
else if(descriptorID==6)//FREAK
{
    cv::FREAK descriptor;
    descriptor.compute(grayObject,objectKeyPoints,
        objectDescriptor);
```

```cpp
        descriptor.compute(grayScene,sceneKeyPoints,
          scenceDescriptor);
    }

    //Construct a brute force matcher object using the
    //Hamming distance as the distance function
    cv::BFMatcher matcher(cv::NORM_HAMMING);
    std::vector< cv::DMatch> matches;
    matcher.match( objectDescriptor, scenceDescriptor,
      matches);

    //Select the best matching points and draw them
    double min_dist = 100;
    for( int i = 0; i < objectDescriptor.rows; i++ )
    {
      double dist = matches[i].distance;
      if( dist < min_dist ) min_dist = dist;
    }
    std::vector< cv::DMatch> good_matches;
    for( int i = 0; i < objectDescriptor.rows; i++ )
    {
      if( matches[i].distance <= 3*min_dist )
      {
        good_matches.push_back( matches[i]);
      }
    }
    drawMatches( grayObject, objectKeyPoints, grayScene,
      sceneKeyPoints,good_matches, result,
      cv::Scalar::all(-1), cv::Scalar::all(-1),
      std::vector<char>(), cv::DrawMatchesFlags::
      NOT_DRAW_SINGLE_POINTS+cv::DrawMatchesFlags::
      DRAW_RICH_KEYPOINTS);
}
```

3. In the activity class, edit `onOptionsItemSelected()` to include the following case:

```java
else if(id==R.id.action_native_match)
{
  if(detectorID==FeatureDetector.HARRIS)
  {
    Context context = getApplicationContext();
    CharSequence text = "Not a valid option for native
      matching";
    int duration = Toast.LENGTH_SHORT;

    Toast toast = Toast.makeText(context, text, duration);
```

```
      toast.show();
      return true;
   }
   if(sampledImage==null || imgToMatch==null)
   {
      Context context = getApplicationContext();
      CharSequence text = "You need to load an object and a
         scene to match!";
      int duration = Toast.LENGTH_SHORT;

      Toast toast = Toast.makeText(context, text, duration);
      toast.show();
      return true;
   }
   Mat finalImg=new Mat();

   FindMatches(imgToMatch.getNativeObjAddr(),
      sampledImage.getNativeObjAddr(),detectorID,
      descriptorID,finalImg.getNativeObjAddr());

   displayImage(finalImg);
}
```

Native matching using ORB for feature detection and description

Stitching two images

Image stitching is the process of finding a correspondence relation between images that already have some degree of overlap.

Usually, the stitching is divided into the following two phases:

- **Image registration and alignment**: Here, we are given two images — one as a source and the other as the target — and the process involves registering the target image spatially to align with the source image. The process can be categorized into intensity-based alignment and feature-based alignment. We will use the feature-based alignment as we are already familiar with the components of this approach (finding, describing, and matching features in two images). The outcome of this process is a motion model with known parameters (that is, a 3x3 homography matrix) that is used to map the coordinates of one image to the other. Once you extend your stitching application to work with more than two images, you will start facing issues related to global registration and finding a globally consistent set of alignment parameters that minimizes the misregistration between all the pairs of images. The techniques used to tackle such issues are bundle adjustment, which improves the estimations by minimizing the reprojection error between every pair of images, and wave correction, which is used to straighten the final result as we typically find a wavy effect in the output of the panorama.

- **Composition**: Once we have all the images aligned and registered, we will need to do exposure correction to the input images so that the blending looks more natural. We will also need to remove visible seams and other stitching artefacts through a process called multi-band blending.

Luckily for us, OpenCV is bundled with a `stitcher` class that will execute the stitching pipeline with a very easy interface; however, **OpenCV4Android** SDK doesn't come with a Java wrapper, and I think that this is another reason why you should be familiar with using the native implementation in your application so that you can extend and add to the current OpenCV Java wrappers in order to fit your needs. So, to work around this, we will add one more function to `Pano.cpp` to call the `stitcher` class and return the result.

UI definitions

We will add a new menu item to execute the native stitching pipeline. Open `res/menu/pano.xml` and add the following item:

```
<item android:id="@+id/action_native_stitcher"
    android:orderInCategory="11"
    android:title="@string/action_native_stitch">
</item>
```

The native stitcher

In this section, we will implement a Java wrapper for the native `stitcher` class so that we can use it in our application:

1. We first declare a new native method in the `activity` class. The native method takes a reference to the first and second scenes and returns an image with the stitching results:

    ```
    public native void Stitch(long sceneOneAddress, long
      sceneTwoAddress,long stitchingResult);
    ```

2. We define the new stitching method in `Pano.cpp`:

    ```
    JNIEXPORTvoid JNICALL
      Java_com_app3_pano_PanoActivity_Stitch(JNIEnv*, jobject,
      jlong sceneOneAddress, jlong sceneTwoAddress,jlong
      stitchingResult) {
      cv::Mat& sceneOne  = *(cv::Mat*)sceneOneAddress;
      cv::Mat& sceneTwo = *(cv::Mat*)sceneTwoAddress;
      cv::Mat& result = *(cv::Mat*)stitchingResult;
      /* The core stitching calls: */
      //a list to store all the images that need to be stitched
      std::vector<cv::Mat> natImgs;
      natImgs.push_back(sceneOne);
      natImgs.push_back(sceneTwo);
      //create a stitcher object with the default pipeline
      cv::Stitcher stitcher = cv::Stitcher::createDefault();
      //stitch and return the result
      stitcher.stitch(natImgs, result);
    }
    ```

3. In the activity class, edit `onOptionsItemSelected` to include the following case:

    ```
    else if(id==R.id.action_native_stitcher)
    {
    if(sampledImage==null || imgToMatch==null)
      {
        Context context = getApplicationContext();
        CharSequence text = "You need to load an two scenes!";
        int duration = Toast.LENGTH_SHORT;

        Toast toast = Toast.makeText(context, text, duration);
        toast.show();
        return true;
      }
      Mat finalImg=new Mat();
    ```

```
      Stitch(imgToMatch.getNativeObjAddr(),
        sampledImage.getNativeObjAddr(),
        finalImg.getNativeObjAddr());
      displayImage(finalImg);
  }
```

Summary

We've seen how to detect, describe, and match different features using both the native and Java wrappers. Additionally, we have seen two applications of image features—one where you can use them to find an object in a scene and the other to stitch two images together in order to build a panorama.

In the next chapter, we will shift gears and touch on the topic of machine learning and how we can use learning algorithms to detect hand gestures, which we can use to build an automatic selfie application.

6
App 4 – Automatic Selfie

In this chapter, we will start working on a new application. The goal of the application is to be able to take a selfie without touching your phone's screen. Your application will be able to detect a certain hand gesture that will trigger the process of saving the current camera frame.

The topics that we will cover will include the following:

- Cascade classifiers used for object detection
- Using OpenCV to manipulate camera frames
- Using a trained cascade classifier to detect objects

Cascade classifiers

In this section, we will discuss the powerful cascade classifier and its components, Haar features, integral images, **Adaptive Boosting** (**Adaboost**), and cascading to build an object detector.

In a nutshell, to construct an object detector, you train it using positive samples (let's say, faces of size 24x24) and negative samples (any other images that are not faces). You keep refining the training process to minimize the training error (the total number of faces classified as non-faces and total number of non-faces classified as faces).

Once the training is done and we get a new image, we ask the detector to check if it has a positive sample (that is, face). The steps followed to do so are as follows:

1. The detector will scan the input image using a scanning window, and every window scanned will get a score.
2. The detector then will say that this window contains a positive sample if its score is greater than a certain threshold; otherwise, it does not.

Haar-like features

Haar-like features are another type of features that are used to detect rigid objects such as faces, pedestrians, and so on.

The *Rapid Object Detection using a Boosted Cascade of Simple Features* paper, by *Paul Viola* and *Michael Jones*, proposed in 2001, introduced the use of Haar-like features with adaptive boosting and cascading to detect faces. Since then, many other features and boosting variations were used to produce classifiers of many other object categories.

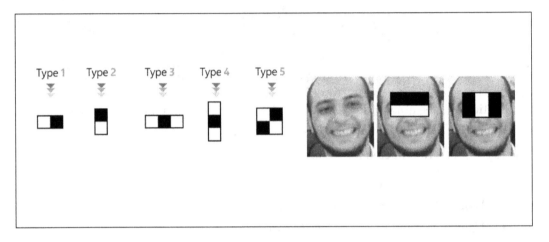

The first step to build a cascade classifier for object detection is try to encode rich information about the positive samples and negative samples as well. In other words, we need to decide which features are considered good enough to separate between, let's say, faces and non-faces. In this section, we will discuss a different type of feature, different from the features that we have seen in *Chapter 5, App 3 - Panoramic Viewer*. The features used here are fixed-size pixel grids, and in this case, no interest point detection is needed because the fixed-size grid defines the description region.

Haar-like features are a fixed-size pixel grid divided into black and white regions, very similar to the convolution kernels that we discussed in *Chapter 2, App 1 - Building Your Own Darkroom*. When you apply the Haar feature to a given image region, you can describe the corresponding image region by subtracting the sum of the pixels' intensities under the white regions from the sum of intensities under the black regions, yielding a single value.

The design of Haar-like features is flexible; for example, you can have several Type 1 features but with different height and/or width applied to different regions of the image. So, given these parameters – feature type (1, 2, 3, 4, or 5), feature width, feature height, and image region on which it is applied – you get a huge pool of features that can be used to describe positive and negative samples.

 In the work of Viola and Jones, the algorithm uses a 24x24 window as the base window size (all the faces and non-faces are resized to 24x24 pixels), and if we consider all the parameters (type, scale, and position), we end up with a pool of size 160,000 features.

The following figure is an example of the features pool:

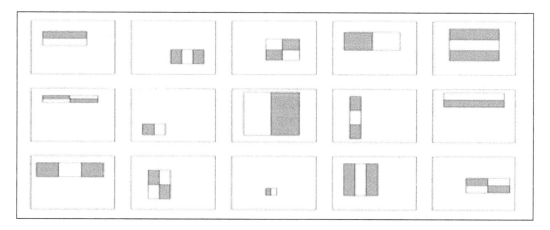

With this huge number of features, applying such an algorithm to a real-time application will be a challenge. So, we need to start doing some optimizations.

One of the optimization techniques that we can use to eliminate the redundant features or select a subset of features that are really discriminate is Adaptive Boosting, and we will get back to the details of this algorithm later in this chapter.

Another optimization technique is used in calculating the feature value (that is, subtracting the white regions from the black regions) and is achieved by calculating what is called the integral image.

The integral image

Whenever we want to calculate the feature value, we need to sum the white patches and subtract them from the black patches, and to do this quickly, Viola and Jones came up with this nice trick called an integral image, as follows:

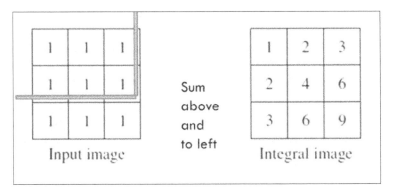

An integral image is an image of the same dimension as the input image, but every integral pixel (i,j) is the sum of all the input pixels that are above and to the left of the input pixel (i,j). For example, when the top left pixel is indexed with (0,0), an integral pixel (1,2) with value **6** is the sum of all the input pixels (i,j), where *i<=1* and *j<=2*.

After calculating the integral image, getting the sum of the input pixels at any region in the image would become an O(1) operation.

For example, consider an integral image with four regions: **A**, **B**, **C**, and **D**. The integral pixel indicated by **1** stores the sum of all the input pixels in region **A**, the integral pixel indicated by **2** is the sum of all the input pixels in regions **A** and **B**, the integral pixel indicated by **3** is the sum of all the input pixels in regions **A** and **C**, and the same for integral pixel **4**, which stores the sum of the input pixels in regions **A**, **B**, **C**, and **D**.

Now, to get the sum of the input pixels in region **D**, you only need the values of the four integral corner pixels 1, 2, 3, and 4, and with a simple arithmetic operation *D=4+1-2-3*, you get the input region sum, as follows:

A   B

•1   •2

C   D

•3   •4

Sum of all pixels in

D = 1+4-(2+3)

$\quad$ = A+(A+B+C+D)-(A+C+A+B)

$\quad$ = D

Adaptive Boosting

Now that we've used the integral image trick to optimize the feature calculation, we need to minimize the number of features to use.

To accomplish this, Viola and Jones used the Adaboost algorithm to select a subset of the relevant features (also known as weak classifiers) that can discriminate between positive and negative samples, as shown in the following image:

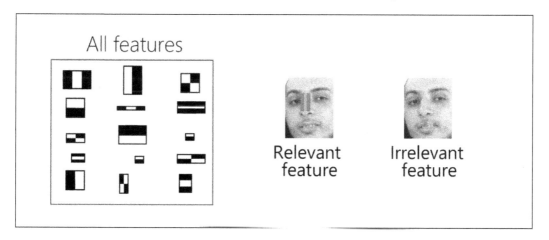

The Adaboost algorithm, in its simplest form, can be described as follows:

1. Start with a uniform weight for the positive and negative samples. All of the samples, positive or negative, are equally important.

2. Iterate over the pool of features/weak classifiers and select the one that will have the lowest weighted classification error.

 A classification error is how many faces are classified as non-faces and how many non-faces are classified as faces using this feature.

3. Increase the weights of the misclassified samples (negative or positive samples) to emphasize the importance of classifying these samples correctly in the next iteration.

4. Repeat steps 2 and 3 until convergence. In many cases, convergence could be by selecting the maximum N number of features.

Once we have the list of these features (weak classifiers), we combine them linearly to form a stronger classifier, which performs better than any individual weak classifier, and finally decide on a threshold that will be used to best separate between the faces and non-faces.

With a new image to classify, we compute N number of relevant features that we select using Adaboost on the input image and decide if it is a face or non-face, based on the selected threshold.

Cascading

One last trick, which gives this type of classifier its name, to speed the detection on any given image is based on the fact that we need to scan the input image with windows of size, let's say, 24x24, similar to that of Viola and Jones's work. However, we know that in many of these windows, the object of interest doesn't exist, so the algorithm will need to be modified in order to reject the negative windows as soon as possible and concentrate on probable positive windows.

To do so, we build a cascade of strong classifiers instead of training one strong classifier. So, all the selected features are grouped into stages where each stage is used to determine whether a given window is definitely a negative window or probably a positive window containing the object of interest. Basically, this update allows us to get rid of a big number of negative windows as early as possible using a smaller set of the relevant features, as follows:

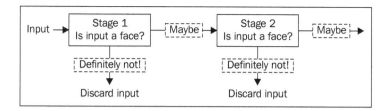

Once the training process is done, we end up with a cascade of strong classifiers that can be applied with a fixed-size sliding window on any given image and detect if the given window contains the object of interest or not:

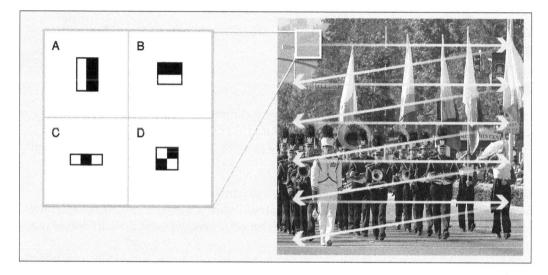

In the next section, we will use an already trained cascade classifier that can detect closed palms in an image, and we will use the presence of the closed palms as a cue to save the current image frame.

Using cascade classifiers to detect objects

In this section, we will use a cascade classifier to detect closed palms in your phone's camera feed, but first, we will have to touch on how to access your phone's camera using OpenCV.

Accessing your phone's camera using OpenCV

We will first create a new application with one blank activity named `AutoSelfie`, following the same steps that we used in the previous chapters.

For the application to access the phone's camera and be able to save pictures, you will need to add the following two permissions in the manifest file:

```
<uses-permissionandroid:name="android.permission.CAMERA"/>
<uses-permissionandroid:name="android.permission.
  WRITE_EXTERNAL_STORAGE"/>
```

You can find the rest of the configurations with the code bundle provided with this chapter.

A camera preview

OpenCV provides a Java implementation for a camera preview class that handles the interaction between the device camera and OpenCV library. The `org.opencv.android.JavaCameraView` class enables the camera to process and draw frames on the device screen.

Up till now, using `JavaCameraView` to preview camera frames was sufficient; however, we will need to define our own camera view class to be able to extend the functionality of the `JavaCameraView` class later on. Now, let's see how to define our own camera view class:

1. Create a new Java class named `com.app4.autodselfie.CamView`.

2. Make the new class extend to `org.opencv.android.JavaCameraView`.

3. Define the `CamView` class constructor as follows:

    ```
    public CamView(Context context, AttributeSet attrs) {
      super(context, attrs);
    }
    ```

This is it. We will get back to this class later when we add the picture-taking functionality to our application.

UI definitions

In the application layout file, `activity_auto_selfie.xml`, we define the main view to be our `CamView` class (as it is a subclass of the `android.view.SurfaceView` class):

```
<LinearLayout xmlns:android="http://schemas.android.com/apk/res/
android"
xmlns:tools="http://schemas.android.com/tools"
android:layout_width="match_parent"
android:layout_height="match_parent">

<com.app4.autoselfie.CamView
android:layout_width="fill_parent"
android:layout_height="fill_parent"
android:id="@+id/auto_selfie_activity_surface_view"/>

</LinearLayout>
```

Previewing the camera frames

Back to the `AutoSelfie` activity, we will follow these steps to start receiving frames from the device's camera:

1. Change the activity class to implement the `CvCameraViewListener2` interface, which will turn the activity class to a listener for three life events of our `CamView` class, camera view start, camera view stop, and camera frame received:

    ```
    public class AutoSelfie extends Activity implements
      CvCameraViewListener2
    ```

2. We declare two empty Mat objects—one to hold the RGB version of the current camera frame and the other to hold the grayscale version:

    ```
    private Mat mRgba;
    private Mat mGray;
    ```

3. We implement the three missing event handlers of `CvCameraViewListener2`. Once the camera view has been started, we initialize the two Mat objects; when the camera view is stopped, we release them, and when we start receiving camera frames, we will return the RGB version of the current frame to be drawn on the screen:

    ```
    public void onCameraViewStarted(int width, int height) {
      mGray = new Mat();
    ```

```
    mRgba = new Mat();
  }

  public void onCameraViewStopped() {
    mGray.release();
    mRgba.release();
  }

  public Mat onCameraFrame(CvCameraViewFrame inputFrame) {
    mRgba=inputFrame.rgba();
    return mRgba;
  }
```

4. Update the `onCreate()` method in order to find the `CamView` object that we defined in the application layout file, set the camera to connect to (frontal or rear) — in our case, we will connect to the frontal camera — and finally, register our activity to be the listener to the `CamView` object life events:

```
mOpenCvCameraView = (CamView)
  findViewById(R.id.auto_selfie_activity_surface_view);
mOpenCvCameraView.setCameraIndex(1);
mOpenCvCameraView.setCvCameraViewListener(this);
```

5. Finally, after loading the OpenCV library successfully, we can enable our `CamView` object to connect to the device camera; only then `onCameraViewStarted()` will be called and the `CamView` object becomes live:

```
private BaseLoaderCallback  mLoaderCallback = new
  BaseLoaderCallback(this) {
  @Override
  public void onManagerConnected(int status) {
    switch (status) {
      case LoaderCallbackInterface.SUCCESS:
      {
        Log.i(TAG, "OpenCV loaded successfully");
        mOpenCvCameraView.enableView();
      } break;
      default:
      {
        super.onManagerConnected(status);
      } break;
    }
  }
};
```

You will notice that the frames drawn are flipped when you hold the device in an upright position; don't worry, we will deal with this issue later.

Detecting closed palms in the camera frames

The next step towards an automatic selfie application is detecting a cue to capture the current camera frame. I found that a closed palm is a good enough cue, and you can consider other cues such as smiling faces and so on.

As we've mentioned in the *Cascade classifiers* section, our detector will be a cascade classifier using Haar-like features.

 The trained stages and selected features are saved in an XML file. You can download the file directly from https://github.com/Aravindlivewire/Opencv/blob/master/haarcascade/aGest.xml, or you can find it in the project folder provided with this chapter.

Using the Java-based cascade classifier

Once you have the trained classifier detecting the object of your choice—in our case, a closed palm—OpenCV provides, out of the box, a multiscale sliding window detector that will run your trained classifier in a sliding window fashion, and on multiple scales of the input image, return the bounding boxes around the detected object at different scales.

 The multiple scales are constructed using the idea of the image pyramid that we encountered in *Chapter 5, App 3 - Panoramic Viewer*.

Using the `org.opencv.objdetect.CascadeClassifier` class as the out-of-the-box sliding window detector is very easy. We first need to copy the trained classifier XML file to the application raw resources folder, `\res\raw\haarhand.xml`.

Next, we declare and initialize the `org.opencv.objdetect.CascadeClassifier` object by changing the `BaseLoaderCallback` implementation as follows:

```
private File cascadeFile;
private CascadeClassifier cascadeClassifier;
private BaseLoaderCallback mLoaderCallback = new
  BaseLoaderCallback(this) {
  @Override
  public void onManagerConnected(int status) {
```

```
      switch (status) {
        case LoaderCallbackInterface.SUCCESS:
        {
          Log.i(TAG, "OpenCV loaded successfully");
          try {
            // load cascade file from application resources
            InputStream is =
              getResources().openRawResource(R.raw.haarhand);
            File cascadeDir = getDir("cascade",
              Context.MODE_PRIVATE);
            cascadeFile = new File(cascadeDir, "haarhand.xml");
            FileOutputStream os = new FileOutputStream(cascadeFile);

            byte[] buffer = new byte[4096];
            int bytesRead;
            while ((bytesRead = is.read(buffer)) != -1) {
              os.write(buffer, 0, bytesRead);
            }
            is.close();os.close();
            //Initialize the Cascade Classifier object using the
            // trained cascade file
            cascadeClassifier = new
            CascadeClassifier(cascadeFile.getAbsolutePath());
            if (cascadeClassifier.empty()) {
              Log.e(TAG, "Failed to load cascade classifier");
              cascadeClassifier = null;
            } else
              Log.i(TAG, "Loaded cascade classifier from " +
                cascadeFile.getAbsolutePath());
            cascadeDir.delete();
          } catch (IOException e) {
            e.printStackTrace();
            Log.e(TAG, "Failed to load cascade. Exception thrown: "
              + e);
          }
          mOpenCvCameraView.enableView();
        } break;
        default:
        {
          super.onManagerConnected(status);
        }
        break;
      }
    }
  };
```

Now, we are ready to process every camera frame to detect the closed palms and take a selfie automatically.

The algorithm that we will use can be summarized as follows:

1. Calculate the minimum size (width and height) of the object that we are looking for. In our case, the minimum size will be 20 percent of the frame size. Of course, you can change the minimum size according to your needs, but be aware that the smaller the object we are looking for, the slower the detection algorithm will run.

2. Run the sliding window detector that we initialized on the current frame to look for the object of interest with the minimum size specified in step 1.

3. Ignore false positive detections. False positive detections occur when the sliding window detector returns a bounding box that doesn't actually contain the object of interest. To minimize the false positives and to stabilize the detection we do the following:

   ° First, we quantize the bounding boxes for every 100 pixels. In other words, we divide the camera frame into 100x100 pixels spatial bucket, and every bounding box is placed in the corresponding spatial bucket depending on its position.

   ° Second, after N frames, we check to see if there is a bucket that contains N bounding boxes. This means that the detection was stable for N consecutive frames, hence the probability that it is a false positive is very low.

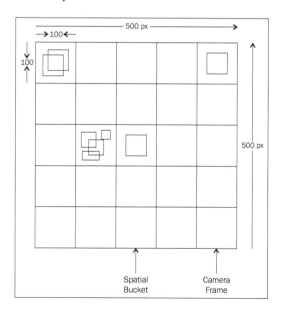

4. Once we have a stable true positive detection (an actual closed palm), we save the current camera frame.

To start implementing this algorithm, we first need to change our CamView class to implement android.hardware.Camera.PictureCallback in order to provide an implementation to the onPictureTaken() callback method to save a given camera frame.

The new CamView class would look as follows:

```java
public class CamView extends JavaCameraView implements
  PictureCallback {
  private static final String TAG = "AutoSelfie::camView";
  private String mPictureFileName;
  public CamView(Context context, AttributeSet attrs) {
    super(context, attrs);
  }

  @Override
  public void onPictureTaken(byte[] data, Camera camera) {
    Log.i(TAG, "Saving a bitmap to file");
    // The camera preview was automatically stopped. Start it
    // again.
    mCamera.startPreview();
    mCamera.setPreviewCallback(this);

    // Write the image in a file (in jpeg format)
    try {
      FileOutputStream fos =
        new FileOutputStream(mPictureFileName);
      fos.write(data);
      fos.close();
    } catch (java.io.IOException e) {
      Log.e("PictureDemo", "Exception in photoCallback", e);
    }
  }

  public void takePicture(final String fileName) {
    Log.i(TAG, "Taking picture");
    this.mPictureFileName = fileName;
    // Postview and jpeg are sent in the same buffers if the
    //queue is not empty when performing a capture.
    // Clear up buffers to avoid mCamera.takePicture to be stuck
    //because of a memory issue
```

```
        mCamera.setPreviewCallback(null);
        // PictureCallback is implemented by the current class
        mCamera.takePicture(null, null, this);
    }
}
```

Once we have the functionality of saving a camera frame ready, we update the AutoSelfie activity class by changing the implementation of onCameraFrame() in order to detect closed palms:

```
public Mat onCameraFrame(CvCameraViewFrame inputFrame) {
    //Flip around the Y axis
    Core.flip(inputFrame.rgba(), mRgba, 1);
    Core.flip(inputFrame.gray(),mGray,1);

    if (mAbsoluteFaceSize == 0) {
        int height = mGray.rows();
        if (Math.round(height * mRelativeFaceSize) > 0) {
            mAbsoluteFaceSize = Math.round(height * mRelativeFaceSize);
        }
    }

    MatOfRect closedHands = new MatOfRect();
    if (cascadeClassifier != null)
        cascadeClassifier.detectMultiScale(mGray, closedHands, 1.1, 2,
            2,new Size(mAbsoluteFaceSize, mAbsoluteFaceSize),
            new Size());

    Rect[] facesArray = closedHands.toArray();
    for (int i = 0; i < facesArray.length; i++)
    {
        Core.rectangle(mRgba, facesArray[i].tl(),
            facesArray[i].br(), HAND_RECT_COLOR, 3);
        Point quatnizedTL=new Point(((int)
            (facesArray[i].tl().x/100))*100,
            ((int)(facesArray[i].tl().y/100))*100);

        Point quatnizedBR=new Point(((int)
            (facesArray[i].br().x/100))*100,
            ((int)(facesArray[i].br().y/100))*100);

        int bucktID=quatnizedTL.hashCode()+quatnizedBR.hashCode()*2;
        if(rectBuckts.containsKey(bucktID))
        {
            rectBuckts.put(bucktID, rectBuckts.get(bucktID)+1);
```

```
      rectCue.put(bucktID, new Rect(quatnizedTL,quatnizedBR));
    }
    else
    {
      rectBuckts.put(bucktID, 1);
    }
  }
  int maxDetections=0;
  int maxDetectionsKey=0;
  for(Entry<Integer,Integer> e : rectBuckts.entrySet())
  {
    if(e.getValue()>maxDetections)
    {
      maxDetections=e.getValue();
      maxDetectionsKey=e.getKey();
    }
  }
  if(maxDetections>5)
  {
    Core.rectangle(mRgba, rectCue.get(maxDetectionsKey).tl(),
      rectCue.get(maxDetectionsKey).br(), CUE_RECT_COLOR, 3);
    SimpleDateFormat sdf =
      new SimpleDateFormat("yyyy-MM-dd_HH-mm-ss");
    String currentDateandTime = sdf.format(new Date());
    String fileName = Environment.
      getExternalStorageDirectory().getPath() +
      "/sample_picture_" + currentDateandTime + ".jpg";

    mOpenCvCameraView.takePicture(fileName);

    Message msg = handler.obtainMessage();
    msg.arg1 = 1;
    Bundle b=new Bundle();
    b.putString("msg", fileName + " saved");
    msg.setData(b);
    handler.sendMessage(msg);
    rectBuckts.clear();
  }
  return mRgba;
}
```

Let's go through the code step by step:

1. We flip the input frame on the y axis to get rid of the mirroring effect:

    ```
    //Flip around the Y axis
    Core.flip(inputFrame.rgba(), mRgba, 1);
    Core.flip(inputFrame.gray(),mGray,1);
    ```

2. Calculate the minimum object size depending on the height of the input frame:

    ```
    if (mAbsoluteFaceSize == 0) {
    int height = mGray.rows();
    if (Math.round(height * mRelativeFaceSize) > 0) {
      mAbsoluteFaceSize = Math.round(height *
        mRelativeFaceSize);}}
    ```

3. We call the `detectMultiScale()` method on the cascade classifier object to build an image pyramid and run a sliding window detector on every scale:

    ```
    MatOfRect closedHands = new MatOfRect();
    if (cascadeClassifier != null)
    cascadeClassifier.detectMultiScale(mGray, closedHands,
      1.1, 2, Objdetect.CASCADE_SCALE_IMAGE,new
      Size(mAbsoluteFaceSize, mAbsoluteFaceSize), new Size());
    ```

    We call `detectMultiScale()` with the following parameters:

    ○   The grayscale version of the camera frame

    ○   An empty `MatOfRect` object to store the detected bounding boxes

    ○   A scale factor to determine how much the input frame is reduced at each scale (*1.1* means reducing the current scale by 10% to construct the next scale in the pyramid; having high values means faster computation at the cost of possibly missing positive detections if the scaling misses the closed palms at certain sizes)

    ○   A minimum neighborhood size to specify how many neighbors each detection should have in order to be retained; otherwise, it will be discarded — this parameter is used to reduce the false positives because true positives tend to have many neighbors detected in the same area due to the use of different scales — a `flagCASCADE_SCALE_IMAGE` to scale the image to build the image pyramid (because there is another approach to detect objects at different scales by scaling the features instead), so for performance gains and simplicity, we will stick with the image pyramid approach that we touched on in *Chapter 5, App 3 - Panoramic Viewer*

    ○   The minimum and maximum size at which we can find the object of interest

4. Once we have the list of detections, we want to group them into spatial buckets of size 100 x 100 pixels to stabilize the detections through different frames and to get rid of the false positives:

```
Rect[] facesArray = closedHands.toArray();
for (int i = 0; i < facesArray.length; i++){
  //draw the unstable detection using the color red
  Core.rectangle(mRgba, facesArray[i].tl(),
    facesArray[i].br(), HAND_RECT_COLOR, 3);
  //group the detections by the top-left corner
  Point quatnizedTL=new Point(((int)
    (facesArray[i].tl().x/100))*100,
    ((int)(facesArray[i].tl().y/100))*100);
  //group the detections by the bottom-right corner
  Point quatnizedBR=new Point(((int)
    (facesArray[i].br().x/100))*100,
    ((int)(facesArray[i].br().y/100))*100);
  //get the spatial bucket ID using the grouped corners
    hashcodes
  int bucktID=
    quatnizedTL.hashCode()+quatnizedBR.hashCode()*2;
  //add or increase the number of grouped detections per
    bucket
  if(rectBuckts.containsKey(bucktID)){
    rectBuckts.put(bucktID, rectBuckts.get(bucktID)+1);
    rectCue.put(bucktID, new
      Rect(quatnizedTL,quatnizedBR));
  }
  else{
    rectBuckts.put(bucktID,1);

  }

}
```

5. We threshold the number of frames that the object is detected in to indicate a stable detection. If the number of frames is greater than the threshold, we save the current frame:

```
int maxDetections=0;
int maxDetectionsKey=0;
for(Entry<Integer,Integer> e : rectBuckts.entrySet()){
  if(e.getValue()>maxDetections){
    maxDetections=e.getValue();
    maxDetectionsKey=e.getKey();
  }
}
```

```
    //Threshold for a stable detection
  if(maxDetections>5){
    //Draw the stable detection in green
    Core.rectangle(mRgba, rectCue.get(
      maxDetectionsKey).tl(), rectCue.get(
      maxDetectionsKey).br(), CUE_RECT_COLOR, 3);
    //build the file name
    SimpleDateFormat sdf = new SimpleDateFormat(
      "yyyy-MM-dd_HH-mm-ss");
    String currentDateandTime = sdf.format(new Date());
    String fileName = Environment.
      getExternalStorageDirectory().getPath()
      +"/sample_picture_" + currentDateandTime + ".jpg";
    //take the picture
    mOpenCvCameraView.takePicture(fileName);
    //show a notification that the picture is saved
    Message msg = handler.obtainMessage();msg.arg1 = 1;
    Bundle b=new Bundle();b.putString("msg", fileName +
      " saved");
    msg.setData(b);handler.sendMessage(msg);
    //clear the spatial buckets and start over
    rectBuckts.clear();
  }
  return mRgba;
}
```

Summary

In this chapter, we built a new application to take automatic selfies based on the famous cascade classifier. We've seen what a cascade classifier is built of starting from the type of features used to the adaptive boosting learning algorithm and cascading. You also learned how to initialize and use a multiscale sliding window-based detector with an already trained classifier to detect closed palm hand gestures and use these detections as cues to capture frames from the device's camera.

Index

A

Adaptive Boosting (Adaboost) 155, 159, 160
Affine transformation 96
Android Developer Tools (ADT) 10
Android NDK
  configuring 11, 12
  downloading 11
  installing 11, 12
  native code building, Eclipse used 12, 13
  URL 11
Android project
  building, OpenCV used 18
  creating, in Android Studio 20-25
  creating, in Eclipse 18
  HelloVisionWorld Android application 18
Android Runtime (ART) virtual machine 14
Android SDK
  URL 9
Application Binary Interface (ABI) 7, 15
averaging filter 66

B

Berkeley Software Distribution (BSD)
  license 1
Binary Robust Independent Elementary
  Features (BRIEF) descriptor 139
Binary Robust Invariant Scalable Keypoints
  (BRISK) descriptor 140

C

Canny edge detector
  about 76
  using 81

cascade classifiers
  about 155
  Adaptive Boosting 159, 160
  cascading 160, 161
  Haar-like features 156, 157
  integral image 158
  used, for detecting objects 161
cascade classifiers, used for detecting
  objects
  camera frames, previewing 163, 164
  camera preview, defining 162
  closed palms detecting, in camera
    frames 165
  Java-based cascade classifier, using 165-172
  phones camera accessing, OpenCV
    used 162
  UI, defining 163
C/C++ Development Tool (CDT) 10

D

digital images
  about 27
  color spaces 28, 29
  Mat class 29

E

Eclipse IDE
  URL 10
edges, finding
  about 73-75
  Canny edge detector 76
  Canny edge detector, using 81, 82
  Sobel edge detector 75
  Sobel filter, applying to edges 77-80
  UI definitions 76

F

FAST corner detector
  about 131
  native FAST, using 133
  UI definitions 132
  using 132
Fast Retina Keypoint (FREAK)
    descriptor 141
feature detectors
  about 117
  Harris corner detector 117
feature matching
  about 141
  object, finding in scene 142-145
  UI definitions 141
flexible perspective correction
  about 105
  applying 106-110
  UI definitions 106

G

Gaussian filter 66, 67
grayscale images
  enhancing 53
  histogram, equalizing 54, 55
  image, converting to 53, 54
  UI definitions 53

H

Haar-like features 156, 157
Harris corner detector
  about 117
  UI definitions 118
  using 118, 119
Hough line transform
  about 83-86
  circles, detecting 92, 93
  circles, drawing 92, 93
  lines, detecting 86-88
  lines, drawing 86-88
  Probabilistic Hough Line Transform 86
  Standard Hough Transform 86
  UI definitions 86, 91
  used, for detecting circles 90, 91

HSV image
  enhancing 55
  histogram, equalizing 56, 57
  UI definitions 56

I

image contrast
  enhancing 51
  grayscale images, enhancing 53
  histogram equalization 52
  histogram, equalizing for grayscale
    image 54
  HSV image, enhancing 55
  image, converting to grayscale 53, 54
  RGB image, enhancing 58
  UI definitions 53
image features 115, 116
image histogram
  about 43
  calculating 43-50
  components 44
images
  loading, to Mat object 33
  reading, OpenCV used 35-42
  stored on phone, processing 33
  UI definitions 34, 35
image smoothing 63
image stitching
  about 152
  native stitcher 153
  UI definitions 152
image transformation
  about 95
  Affine transformation 96
  perspective transformation 96, 97
  rotation 96
  scaled rotation 96
  translation 95, 96
integral image 158

J

Java-based cascade classifier
  using 165-172
Java Native Interface (JNI) 15

Java SE Development Kit 6
    URL 9

L

linear convolution process 65
linear filters 64

M

manual perspective correction
    about 111
    corners, selecting manually 112-114
    UI definitions 112
Mat class
    Mat operations 30-32
Mat object
    image, loading to 33
median filter 68

N

Native Development Kit (NDK)
    about 14, 15
    Android.mk 16, 17
    example 16
    working 14
native feature matching
    about 147
    matching process 148-150
    UI definitions 148
native Harris corner detector
    calling 120
    for Android Studio 123-126
    for Eclipse 120-122
    working on 127-130
noise, removing
    averaging filter 66
    by applying filters 69-73
    Gaussian filter 66, 67
    median filter 68
    UI definitions 68

O

objects
    detecting, cascade classifiers used 161

OpenCV4Android SDK
    URL 13
OpenCV and Android development
        environment, manual installation
    about 9
    ADT and CDT plugins for Eclipse 10
    Android NDK, downloading 11
    Android Studio 9, 10
    Eclipse IDE 10
    Java SE Development Kit 6 9
    OpenCV4Android SDK 13
Open Source Computer Vision (OpenCV) 1
ORB feature detector
    about 135, 136
    native ORB, using 137
    UI definitions 136
    using 136, 137

P

perspective transformation 96, 97

R

RGB image
    histogram, equalizing for image color
        channels 59, 60
    UI definitions 58
rigid perspective correction
    about 97
    estimating, object bounding
        box used 98-104
    UI definitions 97
rotation
    and translation 96
    scaled rotation 96

S

Scale Invariant Feature
        Transform (SIFT) 135
shapes
    detecting 83
    Hough line transform 83-85
    lines detecting, Hough line transform
        used 86
Sobel edge detector 75

spatial filtering
  about 63, 64
  convolution and linear filtering 64, 65
  edges, finding 73
  noise, removing 65
Speeded Up Robust Features (SURF) 135

T

Tegra Android Development Pack (TADP)
  downloading 2-5
  Eclipse, configuring to work with NDK 7
  emulator system images, installing 5, 6
  installing 2
  NDK verification 8
  post-installation configuration 5
  URL 2
translation 95

Thank you for buying
OpenCV Android Programming By Example

About Packt Publishing

Packt, pronounced 'packed', published its first book, *Mastering phpMyAdmin for Effective MySQL Management*, in April 2004, and subsequently continued to specialize in publishing highly focused books on specific technologies and solutions.

Our books and publications share the experiences of your fellow IT professionals in adapting and customizing today's systems, applications, and frameworks. Our solution-based books give you the knowledge and power to customize the software and technologies you're using to get the job done. Packt books are more specific and less general than the IT books you have seen in the past. Our unique business model allows us to bring you more focused information, giving you more of what you need to know, and less of what you don't.

Packt is a modern yet unique publishing company that focuses on producing quality, cutting-edge books for communities of developers, administrators, and newbies alike. For more information, please visit our website at www.packtpub.com.

About Packt Open Source

In 2010, Packt launched two new brands, Packt Open Source and Packt Enterprise, in order to continue its focus on specialization. This book is part of the Packt Open Source brand, home to books published on software built around open source licenses, and offering information to anybody from advanced developers to budding web designers. The Open Source brand also runs Packt's Open Source Royalty Scheme, by which Packt gives a royalty to each open source project about whose software a book is sold.

Writing for Packt

We welcome all inquiries from people who are interested in authoring. Book proposals should be sent to author@packtpub.com. If your book idea is still at an early stage and you would like to discuss it first before writing a formal book proposal, then please contact us; one of our commissioning editors will get in touch with you.

We're not just looking for published authors; if you have strong technical skills but no writing experience, our experienced editors can help you develop a writing career, or simply get some additional reward for your expertise.

Mastering OpenCV Android Application Programming

ISBN: 978-1-78398-820-4   Paperback: 216 pages

Master the art of implementing computer vision algorithms on Android platforms to build robust and efficient applications

1. Understand and utilise the features of OpenCV, Android SDK, and OpenGL.

2. Detect and track specific objects in a video using Optical Flow and Lucas Kanade Tracker.

3. An advanced guide full of real-world examples, helping you to build smart OpenCV Android applications.

Android Application Programming with OpenCV

ISBN: 978-1-84969-520-6   Paperback: 130 pages

Build Android apps to capture, manipulate, and track objects in 2D and 3D

1. Set up OpenCV and an Android development environment on Windows, Mac, or Linux.

2. Capture and display real-time videos and still images.

3. Manipulate image data using OpenCV and Apache Commons Math.

4. Track objects and render 2D and 3D graphics on top of them.

Please check **www.PacktPub.com** for information on our titles

OpenCV Computer Vision Application Programming Cookbook

Second Edition

ISBN: 978-1-78216-148-6   Paperback: 374 pages

Over 50 recipes to help you build computer vision applications in C++ using the OpenCV library

1. Master OpenCV, the open source library of the computer vision community.

2. Master fundamental concepts in computer vision and image processing.

3. Learn the important classes and functions of OpenCV with complete working examples applied on real images.

Learning Image Processing with OpenCV

ISBN: 978-1-78328-765-9   Paperback: 232 pages

Exploit the amazing features of OpenCV to create powerful image processing applications through easy-to-follow examples

1. Learn how to build full-fledged image processing applications using free tools and libraries.

2. Take advantage of cutting-edge image processing functionalities included in OpenCV v3.

3. Understand and optimize various features of OpenCV with the help of easy-to-grasp examples.

Please check **www.PacktPub.com** for information on our titles

www.ingramcontent.com/pod-product-compliance
Lightning Source LLC
Chambersburg PA
CBHW060601060326
40690CB00017B/3783